A LIFE BEYOND AMAZING

A LIFE BEYOND AMAZING

9 DECISIONS THAT WILL
TRANSFORM YOUR LIFE TODAY

DR. DAVID JEREMIAH

W PUBLISHING GROUP

AN IMPRINT OF THOMAS NELSON

CANCEL

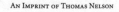

A Life Beyond Amazing
© 2017 David P. Jeremiah

Published in Nashville, Tennessee, by W Publishing Group, an imprint of Thomas Nelson.

Published in association with Yates & Yates, www.yates2.com.

Thomas Nelson titles may be purchased in bulk for educational, business, fund-raising, or sales promotional use. For information, please e-mail SpecialMarkets@ThomasNelson.com.

Unless otherwise noted, Scripture quotations are taken from the New King James Version®. © 1982 by Thomas Nelson. Used by permission. All rights reserved.

Scripture quotations marked KJV are from the King James Version. Public domain.

Scripture quotations marked NIV are from the Holy Bible, New International Version®, NIV®. © 1973, 1978, 1984, 2011 by Biblica, Inc.® Used by permission of Zondervan. All rights reserved worldwide.

Scripture quotations marked NLT are from the Holy Bible, New Living Translation. © 1996, 2004, 2007, 2013, 2015 by Tyndale House Foundation. Used by permission of Tyndale House Publishers, Inc., Carol Stream, Illinois 60188. All rights reserved.

Italics added to Scripture quotations are the author's own emphasis.

ISBN 978-0-7180-8316-8 (eBook)
ISBN 978-0-7852-1619-3 (IE)

Library of Congress Control Number: 2017910352

ISBN 978-0-7180-7990-1

Printed in the United States of America

17 18 19 20 21   LSC   10 9 8 7 6 5 4 3

To David and Barbara Green.
Your lives are beyond amazing.

CONTENTS

INTRODUCTION

At two o'clock on Sunday afternoon, January 8, 2017, a giant fell to the earth, causing the ground to tremble like a palsied hand. One of the best-known giant sequoias, the Pioneer Cabin Tree, collapsed amid California storms. Pioneer Cabin, so named because its hollowed interior was big enough for a home, had pointed upward a thousand years. She was majestic to behold. But her core was gone, her limbs were brittle, her roots were shallow, and only a few branches still clung to life. When lashed by wind and water, the big tree tottered and tumbled and shattered on impact. Her millennium was over.

Many of us are also teetering and tottering, never knowing when the next storm will come. We want to be rooted and solid—a testimony to our Creator. But often we feel hollow, shallow rooted, with no strong core.

What if I told you that you can change all this, that you can weather the storms of life with an inner strength and confidence you've imagined but never felt? What if I told you that you can experience the kind of joy that will change the world around you, and the kind of peace that brings serenity and calmness sweeter than any you've known?

And what if I told you the cost for achieving all of this is free, available to all, and that this special offer will never expire?

Interested?

In this book I share with you how to achieve all that I have described and more. In these pages I show you the path to a life beyond amazing.

No matter who you are, how old, how rich or poor, how tired, disappointed, lonely, or hopeless—you can follow this path. No matter what difficulty and pain life has dealt you, or what riches and opportunities you feel it hasn't, this path is for you.

This book is about character. It's about how we develop the character that Christ wants for us, that God makes us capable of achieving, and that the Holy Spirit is always, always ready to guide us to. I want to help you develop character qualities beyond the norm. I want to show you how to build a life beyond amazing, and, in so doing, make an impact beyond imagination.

SET FEAR ASIDE

You don't need fear anymore. You need new hope, new strength, and new understanding. You need a fresh start on a new path.

And what does our world need? Our world needs solid-to-the-core people with unimpaired grit and unimpeded godliness. The church needs a rekindling of the nine traits that go to the core of character and are called the "fruit of the Spirit" in Galatians 5:22–23. God wants us to be people of love and joy and peace. He wants to build endurance into our lives and instill in us compassion for those who need our help. He is ready to bestow the qualities of champions—generosity, integrity, humility, and self-discipline.

People with those qualities are saints for all seasons.

They are people like Jesus.

This book is a manual on how to develop these qualities. You alone can make the decision to pursue this life, and if you do, I promise you will not be alone. Not ever.

The qualities of a life beyond amazing are produced within us by the Holy Spirit. It is His love, joy, peace, endurance, compassion, generosity, integrity, humility, and self-discipline you seek. These qualities represent the essence of the personality of Jesus Himself. When the Spirit of Christ comes to live within us, He reproduces Himself, putting these traits at our core so we can achieve godly character. Our first step, then, is our commitment to Christ and our willingness to grow in understanding of how the Holy Spirit works in us.

IT'S UP TO YOU

This is a life-changing choice. Yes, you will have almighty help, but the work will still be up to you. These nine qualities require commitment and effort. Think of them as representing nine decisions that will transform your life if you take them seriously. And if you do take them seriously, you will start a journey that will not leave you as the same person you are today.

The same Bible that describes love as a fruit of the Spirit also commands us to love one another, to clothe ourselves with love, and to walk in love. The same New Testament that calls joy a by-product of the Spirit also tells us to rejoice in the Lord always and to be of good cheer.

Lots of extra joy doesn't sound so difficult, does it? Plenty of love to fill your heart and your life is the kind of commitment you're more than ready to make, right?

That depends. None of what I will share with you is beyond your reach . . . unless you try it alone, without the spiritual support Jesus makes available to us. That spiritual support will sustain you when what I'm asking you to do feels like more than you can handle, much less achieve. I will tell you how to access that support and how you will be uplifted for any challenge when you do. Because if you take this path and do this work, you will have help. Not just any help, you will have the help of the Holy Spirit every step of the way. And nothing, truly nothing, is more powerful than that.

In John 10:10, the Lord said, "I have come that they may have life, and that they may have it more abundantly." The abundant life is solid to the core, fruitful to the end, and amazing to experience. It is the biblical norm for God's people.

In Philippians 2:13, we read: "*It is God who works in you* both to will and to do for His good pleasure." The development of character is a joint effort by our Savior and ourselves, and it is part and parcel of the abundant life.

Why, then, are we living beneath the norm?

Why is there such a gap between what Christ wants us to be and what we are?

THREE REASONS WE STRUGGLE

Sometimes it's because we misunderstand the nature of salvation.

Salvation is one of the Bible's great words, but many don't understand that the Bible presents salvation in three stages. The moment we truly receive Christ as Savior and Lord, we are instantly and eternally saved from the *penalty* of sin. During our Christian life spans on earth, we're gradually being saved from the *power* of sin and should grow in godliness. One day in heaven, we will be saved from the very *presence* of sin and will be wholly glorified.

Many people consider salvation a onetime, past event. They forget its ongoing nature.

N. T. Wright wrote:

> Many Christians . . . have a big gap in their vision of what being a Christian is all about. It's as though they were standing on one side of a deep, wide river, looking across to the further bank. On *this* bank you declare your faith. On the *opposite* bank is the ultimate result—final salvation itself. But what are people supposed to do in the meantime? Simply stand here and wait? Is there no bridge between the two? . . .
>
> The bridge in question goes by many names. . . . But one of the most obvious names is *character.* . . . the transforming, shaping, and marking of a life and its habits.[1]

From the first step of that process to our last breath, we are crossing this bridge. Throughout our lives, we develop our character consciously or unconsciously. In your journey to a life beyond amazing, you will learn to develop your character in ways that bring remarkable rewards.

There's a second reason people miss the abundant life: they misapply the concept of works. Many biblical passages teach that we're not saved by our own efforts but by the grace of God alone. But the same passages also tell us good works are an essential evidence of the salvation experience.

For example, Ephesians 2:8–9 says, "For by grace you have been saved through faith, and that not of yourselves; it is the gift of God, not of works, lest anyone should boast." Hallelujah for that!

But the next verse says, "For we are His workmanship, created in Christ Jesus for good works, which God prepared beforehand that we should walk in them" (Eph. 2:10).

Hallelujah for that too! We are not saved *by* good works, but *for* good works. God saves us and leaves us on earth for a span so we can serve Him here, letting our light shine before others, so they can see our good works and glorify our Father in heaven (Matt. 5:16).

If you choose to take the path I will show you, this understanding will be a blessing. Again and again we will discuss what you can actually *do* to achieve this new life. It begins with God's grace, and it is sustained by His grace as you shape your character by what you do as you cross the bridge.

A third reason we fail to develop godly character involves a mistaken view of spirituality. Some believe we have little or no role in our own Christian maturity. God does everything, they think, and we simply have to "let go and let God." After all, if it's the "fruit of the Spirit," we should passively let Him work within us as we abide in Christ.

It's true the Holy Spirit alone can reproduce the character of our Lord Jesus, and we must always abide in Christ. But the Bible also makes us active partners in the process, and we must be diligent to do our part. "Be diligent to present yourself approved to God, a worker who does not need to be ashamed" (2 Tim. 2:15).

Diligent is not a word for the fainthearted. It implies consistency, self-discipline, making every effort, and working with great conscientiousness.

Bono, the lead singer of U2, described his experience of spiritual growth like this:

Your nature is a hard thing to change; it takes time. . . . I have heard of people having life-changing, miraculous turn-arounds, people set free from addiction after a single prayer, relationships saved where both parties "let go, and let God." But it was not like that for me. For all that "I was lost, I am found," it is probably more accurate to say, "I was really lost. I'm a little less so at the moment." And then a little less and a little less again. That to me is the spiritual life. The slow reworking and rebooting of a computer at regular intervals, reading the small print of the service manual. It has slowly rebuilt me in a better image. It has taken years, though, and it is not over yet.[2]

Bono is saying his spiritual progress since conversion has taken time and effort to achieve. He's also saying that his work isn't done yet, and he has no expectation of perfection anytime soon.

God has given us everything we need for life and godliness. And He has given us the indwelling strength and guidance of the Holy Spirit. The rest is up to us.

Peter says, "Giving all diligence, add to your faith virtue, to virtue knowledge, to knowledge self-control, to self-control perseverance, to perseverance godliness, to godliness brotherly kindness, and to brotherly kindness love" (2 Peter 1:5–7).

PARTNERING WITH GOD

As I pondered this, I came across a short essay that made it all as practical as putting on our shoes or rolling up our sleeves. Pat Goggins wrote:

I describe Character as the only thing that goes in the casket with you. It's the only thing you take with you to the hereafter. . . .

Character is returning extra change at the grocery store. Character is keeping appointments and being on time, honoring your commitments and honoring your word. Character is choosing the harder right instead of the easier wrong. Character is setting priorities that honor God, family, country, and then career.

Character in marriage is working through the tough times. . . . Character is being committed to the well-being of your family and friends, associates, and others, even if it is personally costly; and yes, Character is setting a good example.

A married person of Character acts married all the time. A person of Character is self-disciplined and self-controlled. Character implies the courage to stand for what is right, if necessary, all alone to oppose what is wrong and to make the effort to discern the difference. Character is being truthful in all things while being sensitive to the fact that sometimes the truth hurts and need not be spoken.[3]

Do you want to be a person like that? I'm sure you do, and so do I. That's the way we should be whenever we enter a room, go to a meeting, compete in a game, hug our spouses, tuck our children into bed, get on an airplane, check into a hotel, make a purchase, or react to adversity.

That's what God desires for us too. He wants us to be trees that never topple, giants that never fall, people who bear enduring fruit. The Bible says:

> "Blessed is the man who trusts in the LORD,
> And whose hope is the LORD.

For he shall be like a tree planted by the waters,

Which spreads out its roots by the river,

And will not fear when heat comes;

But its leaf will be green,

And will not be anxious in the year of drought,

Nor will cease from yielding fruit." (Jer. 17:7–8)

The ninefold fruit of the Spirit in Galatians 5 is a gift of God, but don't forget: it also represents nine decisions on your part. Those decisions will affect you every day; they will transform you into a person of character who fulfills your God-given potential and inspires others to do the same.

It's amazing to meet people like that.

It's beyond amazing to be one.

CHAPTER 1

A LIFE OF LOVE

Love is not about what we feel for others—
it's about what we do for others.

Who gets married on a Tuesday?

That's what family and friends of Kim and Scotti Madison wondered when they opened their invitations to the couple's Tuesday wedding. But to Kim and Scotti, it made perfect sense.

Kim lived in Nashville, where she'd raised her five children after a tough divorce. Scotti, also divorced, traveled to Nashville on business. Friends introduced them, and from the day they met, they shared a commitment to taking things slowly and making sure any relationship that developed would be prayerfully considered.

"When I was navigating the dating world after my divorce, my pastor said, 'Kim, the right man for you is the one who would be serving the homeless whether you are there or not,'" Kim recalled.

Sure enough, the night Scotti traveled to Nashville to ask Kim to consider dating him seriously was also the night she'd committed to overseeing midweek worship at the Nashville Women's Mission. She said yes to the date, on the condition that Scotti join her at the mission. And, she added, since he'd be coming anyway, would he be her guest speaker?

Scotti agreed, and that night he spoke from his heart to the women about losing his son to heroin and about living a strong life in the aftermath of such a tragedy.

"I heard his heart for Jesus, and I saw his desire to serve others," Kim said. "I knew that night God wanted us to be together."

Not long after that night, they were invited to volunteer at the Bridge Ministry, a thirteen-year-old ministry serving the homeless under the Jefferson Street Bridge in Nashville.

"This was a sector of our society I used to look through and around," Scotti says. "Now I look into the eyes and souls of those who are hurting. Jesus said, 'They will know you by your love.' Serving, listening, hugging, and praying with these special people alongside Kim is where I am the happiest and most fulfilled."

By Christmas, Scotti made it clear he wanted to marry Kim, and she felt the same way about him. Over the following month, the couple prayed about God's timing for the wedding and the details. Of course, Nashville offered plenty of beautiful venues, and there were a number of Fridays and Saturdays that would have worked just fine.

But that's not what God showed them. Both Kim and Scotti felt the Lord showed them the same location and time: under the Jefferson Street Bridge, on a Tuesday night, when they could celebrate with and serve the homeless.

"It was a real destination wedding," Scotti says, smiling. "And we shared it with our special guests—those whom Jesus wanted invited to the wedding banquet: 'the poor, the crippled, the lame, the blind.'"

"We'd reached a point in our lives where we recognized Christ's love is centered around serving," Kim adds. "We wanted our friends and family to know and hear, 'This is who we are. Will you now serve alongside us?'"

And so, on May 9, 2017, they gathered with their guests, including more than two hundred of their homeless friends. Everyone enjoyed an amazing meal, a worship service and a heartfelt ceremony. Knowing that to the homeless a slice of wedding cake meant they were truly guests who mattered, Kim and Scotti made sure everyone had all the wedding cake they wanted. When Kim and Scotti were pronounced man and wife, they went down every aisle and greeted their guests individually.

No one who attended that wedding left unmoved or unchanged. Why? Because Kim and Scotti took the love that filled their hearts when they served the homeless, and they gave it back—bestowing it abundantly and permanently on every one of their wedding guests.

WHAT IS LOVE?

Is there a more complex word than *love*? I don't think so. We talk about loving God, loving football, loving pizza, receiving love, giving love, and making love. At church we sing about the love of God that's "greater far than tongue or pen can ever tell."

Then we get in the car and head home, radio on, listening to songs about love: selfish and self-centered love; one-sided, hopeless love; deceit and cruelty masquerading as love; and once in a while, a mature, other-centered love that stands the test of time.

No wonder we take the word *love* for granted! We're obsessed with it, yet rarely do we witness or hear what love truly is in the world around us.

If true love is so unfamiliar, why do people write, talk, text, and sing about it so much?

Because there's a hole in the human heart. We're desperate for the experience of genuine love. Within intimate relationships and in our daily interactions with others, every one of us needs reassurance, affection, and fellowship—all forms of love. Love is oxygen for the soul; we have to have it. The first thing an infant needs at birth is to be held tenderly, to literally feel loved. This manifestation of love brings a lifetime of blessings.

The Bible has a lot to say about love. In the New International Version of the Bible, the word *love* occurs 567 times. From the book of Genesis to the book of Revelation, the story of the Bible is the story of God's unconditional and relentless love for mankind. Love is the foundation of everything good, which is why I chose it to be the first chapter in this book. Quite simply, love is what makes every other part of a life beyond amazing possible.

The love that appears at the top of almost every list of virtues in the Bible is not just God's love for us, but also our love for one another. To become a Christian means the very love of God is poured into your heart; it grows within you just as grapes grow on a vine, for the fruit of the Spirit is love.

This love isn't just a spiritual sensation. This love wears work gloves and handles the everyday nuts and bolts of life. It's highly practical. It hugs the lonely, feeds the hungry, tends the sick, comforts the sorrowful, and puts up with the insufferable. It is kind and long-suffering, pure and perceptive, positive in outlook. It is truly the key ingredient of a life beyond amazing.

THE HIGHEST FORM OF LOVE

Until Jesus came to earth, this kind of love was unknown. The world's concept of love was self-centered, love that demanded something in return. But when God sent His Son as a love-gift to this world, His special, other-centered love was put on display for all to see. And this love was so different from anything anyone had seen before that it was given a special name. They called it *agape.*

Agape is unconditional, divine love, the kind of love God exercises toward mankind. At the heart of *agape* is sacrifice. It is not the spontaneous, impulsive love we see on television and in the movies. It is the reasoning, esteeming, and choosing type of love. *Agape* is the highest form of love—the love everyone wants to receive but few seem ready to give because of the sacrifice involved.

Most of us know the story of *Beauty and the Beast,* but you may not have considered the kind of love it describes. The eighteenth-century fairy tale tells of a handsome young prince made ugly by a fairy after he refused hospitality to her during a storm. Trapped in the form of a hideous beast, he lives alone, desperate to avoid the disgust on the faces of those who see him. The Beast can only be restored to his original form if someone loves him truly, in spite of his horrible appearance. One day Beauty appears and, ultimately, offers him that kind of redeeming, transforming love.

G. K. Chesterton wrote that the great lesson of *Beauty and the Beast* is that "a thing must be loved before it is lovable."[1]

This is a wonderful, familiar example of God's *agape*—the highest form of love. We are made unlovely by our sin, yet God's love sees beneath it the person He created. When we open ourselves to His love, it transforms us back into what we were meant to be.

One of the best definitions of *agape* I've ever heard is this: "It is the power to move us toward another person with no expectation of reward."[2]

Wouldn't it be amazing if Christians were as obsessed with God's brand of love as society is obsessed with the world's concept of love? In this chapter we will learn much about God's love for us, and we will see how God's love for us is the key to our loving one another.

THE COMMAND TO LOVE

I heard about a teenager who was asked what she thought love was and she answered, "Love is a feeling you feel when you feel that what you feel is a feeling you never felt before." That's how most of us think of love. As a feeling. A feeling is something that just happens to us, brought on by circumstances beyond our control. We can't help who we love—and, by extension, who we *don't* love.

But in the Bible, love is not just a feeling. It's not just one option among many. It's a command. Jesus says: "A new *commandment* I give to you, that you love one another" (John 13:34) and "This is My *commandment*, that you love one another as I have loved you" (John 15:12).

Over and over in the New Testament, God's people are commanded to love, in different contexts and different settings, and as parents, children, and individuals. And on thirteen occasions Christians are commanded to "love one another." Why is that? We shouldn't have to be commanded to love our brothers and sisters in Christ; it should just come naturally, right? And who would really know if we *didn't* love one another? Of course, God would know, but the Bible tells us that the world will also know: "By this all will know that you are My disciples, if you have love for one another" (John 13:35).

The world is watching us, waiting to see if this Jesus thing really makes a difference. And when the world senses hypocrisy, it will pounce.

How do we know if we're truly loving one another? Because love is not about what we *feel* for others—it's about what we *do* for others. The true power of love is found in selfless attitudes and actions that seek the best for another person without expecting anything in return. When we act in that way, the feeling of love follows close behind.

When the apostle John records Jesus' indictment against the church in Ephesus in Revelation 2, we see this concept at work: "Nevertheless I have this against you, that you have left your first love" (v. 4).

This dynamic, first-century church had started out with such passion for the Lord Jesus and such determination to make a difference in their city. Along the way, something happened. Their passion diminished, and they developed indifference toward the Lord and His purposes for their lives.

What solution did Jesus offer? Among other things, He told them to go back and "do the first works" (v. 5). They were told to return to the actions of their early experience, and in doing so they would recover their passion. In other words, *act* as though they were filled with passion for the Lord, *act* as if they were determined to make a difference in their city through the love of Jesus Christ.

The world constantly tells us to follow our hearts. What they really mean is to follow our feelings. But God's kind of love— *agape*—doesn't follow. It leads by example. Love is a verb. It acts. It leads our hearts and changes lives.

In his book *Caring and Commitment*, Lewis Smedes told the story of James Ettison's love for his wife, Alice:

> They got married, and settled snugly . . . into happiness. But about two years later, on a cold November night before the snow had come, Alice's car skidded on a stretch of ice that had formed un-noticed beneath a bridge on a two-way stretch of highway, and she ran head on, full speed, into a car coming from the other direction.
>
> Alice survived. After tilting toward death for a year, she gave signs of living again, and she did. But she was never the same. She was all but paralyzed from the hips downward. Her memory was spotty and selective, and she uttered sounds that James had to learn to translate the way a person learns a new language. As months slithered into years, the past crept back with fits and starts into Alice's memory, which, in some ways, made life harder for her, because then she became that much more conscious of her other handicaps. She bore them like a smiling angel most of the time, but unpredictably, out of the blue, she sometimes, for weeks on end, was smothered by depression.
>
> James quit his traveling job right after the accident, got some work near home, and made a nearly full-time vocation of taking care of Alice. . . . Nobody ever heard a discouraging word from his corner. . . .
>
> Alice died fifteen years or so after that one terrible November night, and somebody asked James how he had done it all so patiently when he had gotten such a poor smidgen of everything he had hoped Alice would give to him. He said he had never thought to ask, though he had sometimes asked God why Alice was stuck with living and got nothing back from it.
>
> But, pressed a little, he said it: "I just loved her."[3]

A GIFT THAT REQUIRES HARD WORK

The concept of love poses a major question for those of us who follow Christ. Is this love a gift from God we receive when we experience salvation, or is it something we're responsible for developing after we believe? The answer to both questions is yes. Yes, this love is a gift from God, imparted to us by the Holy Spirit:

- "The love of God has been poured out in our hearts by the Holy Spirit who was given to us" (Rom. 5:5).
- "For God has not given us a spirit of fear, but of power and of love and of a sound mind" (2 Tim. 1:7).

And yes, Christians are called to cultivate love with determination and diligence.

Paul summarized his description of love in 1 Corinthians 13 with this: "And now abide faith, hope, love, these three; but the greatest of these is love" (v. 13). Because of the chapter divisions we find in our modern Bibles (added in the thirteenth century for ease of use), we assume at this point that Paul has finished his discussion of love, but he hasn't.

The first words of chapter 14?

"Pursue love."

Two simple words summarize one of the toughest assignments we're given as followers of Christ:

Loving people is about the most difficult thing that some of us do. We can be patient with people and even just and charitable, but how are we supposed to conjure up in our hearts that warm, effervescent sentiment of goodwill which the New Testament

9

calls "love"? Some people are so miserably unlovable. That odorous person with the nasty cough who sat next to you in the train, shoving his newspaper into your face, those crude louts in the neighborhood with the barking dog, that smooth liar who took you in so completely last week—by what magic are you supposed to feel toward these people anything but revulsion, distrust and resentment, and justified desire to have nothing to do with them?[4]

But the command is not ambiguous. We are called to love. "Here we have a prime example of that seeming paradox that stands at the center of the Christian life. . . . the fruit is always a gift, but it still requires hard work."[5]

Since love is both a gift and a task, what is the work we need to do if we desire to live this life beyond amazing? How can we become more loving people?

PURSUE GENUINE LOVE

Henry Drummond preached a classic message on love, titled "The Greatest Thing in the World," in which he said, "If a piece of ordinary steel is attached to a magnet and left there, after a while the magnetism of the magnet passes into the steel so that it too becomes a magnet."[6] As we stay attached to Jesus, His love will pass into us and out to others.

When we receive God's love into our hearts, it creates a reservoir of love we can draw from when we need to love someone. In other words, we love others with the same love with which we ourselves have been loved!

That reservoir of love is pure, and when we "do the first things" and act as if we love, it fills our hearts. Acting as though we love others and then sincerely opening ourselves to be filled with God's pure love is different from just pretending we love everyone. Don't fake it and tell yourself you're done. That kind of so-called love is not what God requires of us, and He sees through it, even when we're blind to it.

With tongue in cheek, Pastor Ray Ortlund wrote:

> The beautiful "one another" commands of the New Testament are famous. But it is also striking to notice the "one anothers" that do not appear there.
>
> For example, sanctify one another, humble one another, scrutinize one another, pressure one another, embarrass one another, corner one another, interrupt one another, defeat one another, sacrifice one another, shame one another, marginalize one another, exclude one another, judge one another, run one another's lives, confess one another's sins. . . .
>
> Our relationships with one another reveal to us what we really believe as opposed to what we *think* we believe, our convictions as opposed to our opinions. It is possible for the gospel to remain at the shallow level of opinion, even sincere opinion, without penetrating to the deeper level of conviction. But when the gospel grips us down in our convictions, we embrace its implications wholeheartedly. Therefore, when we mistreat one another, our problem is not a lack of surface niceness but a lack of gospel depth. What we need is not only better manners but, far more, true faith.[7]

Obviously this was as much of a problem in the New Testament era as it is today. The writers of the epistles constantly drove home the importance of authenticity in the believer's relationships with others.

- "Since you have purified your souls in obeying the truth through the Spirit in *sincere love* of the brethren, love one another fervently with a pure heart" (1 Peter 1:22).
- "But whoever has this world's goods, and sees his brother in need, and shuts up his heart from him, how does the love of God abide in him? My little children, *let us not love in word or in tongue, but in deed and in truth*" (1 John 3:17–18).
- "Now the purpose of the commandment is *love from a pure heart, from a good conscience, and from sincere faith*" (1 Tim. 1:5).

REFLECT ON GOD'S LOVE FOR YOU

The apostle John wrote: "By this we know love, because He laid down His life for us. And we also ought to lay down our lives for the brethren. . . . Beloved, if God so loved us, we also ought to love one another" (1 John 3:16; 4:11).

On October 22, 2007, the first Medal of Honor awarded for combat in Afghanistan was presented to the family of Lt. Michael Murphy, a Navy SEAL who gave his life to make a radio call for help for his team. Murphy, who was not yet thirty, was only the fourth Navy SEAL to earn the Medal of Honor since the Vietnam War.

In June 2005, Murphy and three other SEALs were sent on a mission into the rugged Afghan mountains to search for a known terrorist. They encountered local tribesmen who reported them to the Taliban. Murphy's team was trapped by scores of enemy troops who surrounded them on three sides and forced them into a ravine. Soon all four men had sustained injuries. "We were hurtin'," said the team's sole survivor, Petty Officer 2nd Class Marcus Luttrell. "We were out of ammo, and . . . it was bad, it was real bad."

Murphy moved from man to man to keep his team together, though he had to expose himself to enemy fire to do so. Then, because the mountainous terrain blocked communications, he made the decision to move into an open area to call for help. Already wounded, and despite incoming fire, he provided his unit's location and information about the opposing force. While making the call, he took two more rounds and dropped the handset but managed to retrieve it and complete the call. He even said thank you at the end of the transmission.[8]

Petty Officer Luttrell survived the firestorm because he was blasted over the ridge by a rocket-propelled grenade and was knocked unconscious. When he came to, he hid in a rock crevice, staunching his bleeding wounds with mud. Almost a week later, after being taken in by local villagers who refused to turn him over to the Taliban, he was rescued.

Marcus Luttrell came home determined to tell the story of that day. His book, *Lone Survivor,* became a movie of the same name, ensuring that Lt. Michael Murphy and the rest of his team are never forgotten.

There's only one symbol I know greater than the Medal of Honor, and that's the Cross of Calvary. For a moment, use your imagination to consider how similar our plight was to that of Murphy's team—trapped by the enemy, outnumbered, wounded, and facing overwhelming odds. Yet one man, Jesus, stood up and stretched out His arms and saved us.

Years ago, when my wife and I were in London, we visited some of the great churches in that city. As we were leaving St. Paul's Cathedral, I saw a statue in the annex that I've never forgotten. It was a huge portrayal of Jesus Christ twisting in anguish on the cross, intense pain on His face and blood dripping down His body. Underneath was a plaque reading: "This is how God loved the world."

Only when we understand how much God has loved us will we be able to love one another as we've been commanded. God calls us to be imitators of His love: "Therefore be imitators of God as dear children. And walk in love, as Christ also has loved us and given Himself for us" (Eph. 5:1–2).

PRAY FOR GREATER LOVE

One of the most productive things we can do to pursue a life beyond amazing is to read Paul's prayers for the churches he was involved with. He didn't pray for greater attendance, bigger offerings, or even more people becoming Christians. When we examine his prayers, we discover something far more challenging.

For instance, to the Christians in Philippi, he said this: "And this I pray, that your love may abound still more and more in knowledge and all discernment" (Phil. 1:9).

And for the believers in Ephesus, this was his prayer: "That He would grant you, according to the riches of His glory, to be strengthened with might through His Spirit in the inner man, that Christ may dwell in your hearts through faith; that you, being rooted and grounded in love, may be able to comprehend with all the saints what is the width and length and depth and height—to know the love of Christ which passes knowledge; that you may be filled with all the fullness of God" (Eph. 3:16–19).

In 1 Corinthians 11:1, Paul urges his readers to imitate him. We too should pray for greater love, whether we're praying that prayer for others or for ourselves. It is God's desire for all of us that we continue to grow in our ability to love one another. I promise you this is a prayer He will surely answer.

Having been a pastor for almost fifty years, I can also promise you there will always be people who test your ability to love. Some people are harder to love than others. Here's an important point to remember: You don't have to like them, but you do have to love them as Christ tells you to. Loving these people is a decision you make. Once you've made that decision, then you do good things for them because that's how you express your love.

One time I was in the drive-through line at the McDonald's near our church. I didn't realize that when I was pulling into the line, I'd cut a woman off. But when she rolled down her window and started swearing at me, I got the message loud and clear.

We all know what it's like to be yelled at furiously for something we did accidentally. So when I reached the window, I knew I had to do something to close this incident in a positive way. I told the cashier I wanted to pay for the meal of the woman in the car behind me. Sure enough, immediately I felt better. I don't know if she felt better, but I know I did.

Another time, the station manager of a radio station that aired our show called and said he was taking my show off to put someone else's show in our time slot. The details don't matter; but it was not a just or good decision, and it got into my spirit. I knew I needed to act to relieve myself of the burden this was putting on my heart. So I asked God for guidance, and He showed me what to do.

We'd paid for our airtime in advance, and some of that money was still in my account at that radio station. I called the station and told them not to send me that money, but to put it in the other man's account to pay for his time.

As soon as I did that, the whole incident was behind me. It was over. I put a period at the end of that sentence, turned the page, and left it behind.

The Bible says when others treat you badly, you're supposed to love them, pray for them, bless them, and do good things for them. If you can't do it because you want to, then you must do it because you're obedient.

Interestingly, the story doesn't end there. About six months later, the station manager called again. He was putting us back on the air in an even better time slot. And in that new time slot we did even better than before!

LOVE YOUR ENEMY

Difficult, unpleasant people are one thing. An enemy is something very different.

It may be one of the most difficult things we are called to do in this life, but Jesus very clearly commands us to love our enemies. "You have heard that it was said, 'You shall love your neighbor and hate your enemy.' But I say to you, love your enemies, bless those who curse you, do good to those who hate you, and pray for those who spitefully use you and persecute you, that you may be sons of your Father in heaven" (Matt. 5:43–45).

If you are still in doubt about the fact that love is an action, take note of this verse. Jesus tells us to love our enemies, and then He tells us how: bless them, do good to them, and pray for them. That's how you love your enemy.

To the natural mind, this seems to be taking love a step too far. How can you love people who are undermining values you hold dear? How can you love the person who lied about you to make herself look good? Or the person who claimed your idea as his own and got a promotion for it? Or the person who stole your identity, molested your daughter, or murdered your son?

This is truly where we must be kind to ourselves and very clear about what God is asking us to do. We are not asked to abandon our feelings; we are asked to bless and pray that God will do His work in the lives of our enemies. We are not asked to expose ourselves or others to these people, but only to pray, bless, and do good for them. After all, many of those who harm us are not repentant, and they may even still be a danger or threat to us or others in some way.

This is an enormous task, and it may seem impossible. And that is why we have examples in the Bible of people who obeyed this command.

Jesus gave us the ultimate example by giving up His life on the cross for the very people who were demanding and performing His execution, and then saying from the cross, "Father, forgive them, for they do not know what they do" (Luke 23:34). And His followers took that example to heart.

When Stephen was being stoned to death for preaching the gospel, he also asked God to forgive his executioners: "Then he knelt down and cried out with a loud voice, 'Lord, do not charge them with this sin'" (Acts 7:60).

The apostle Paul spent his adult life as a servant of the gospel and was beaten, whipped, rebuked, and despised for it: "Being reviled, we bless; being persecuted, we endure; being defamed, we entreat" (1 Cor. 4:12–13). In his letter to the Romans, Paul said, "'If your enemy is hungry, feed him; if he is thirsty, give him a drink;

for in so doing you will heap coals of fire on his head.' Do not be overcome by evil, but overcome evil with good" (Rom. 12:20–21).

During the American Revolution, a pastor named Peter Miller was opposed and humiliated by Michael Whitman, an evil-minded man who did all he could to suppress the gospel. One day, Mr. Whitman was arrested for treason and sentenced to die. Rather than breathe a sigh of relief at the news, Peter Miller traveled seventy miles on foot to plead for his enemy's life. When General George Washington first listened to the plea, he told Miller that he would not grant the life of his friend. At that the pastor leaped to his feet. "My friend!" he exclaimed. "Michael Whitman is not my friend, but my bitterest enemy!" Washington changed his mind and granted a pardon. Peter Miller was doing exactly what Jesus called us to do. He was loving his enemy, not in how he felt toward the man, but in what he did for the man.[9]

DON'T BE AFRAID TO RISK

One reason people give for withholding love from others is that they don't want to get hurt. They talk about the times when they loved and were wounded in return. "I'll never trust anyone again," they say. "I'll never let anyone hurt me like that again."

If you've experienced rejection or have walked through it with others, I understand your determination never to risk that happening again. But read this before you make that decision.

To love at all is to be vulnerable. Love anything, and your heart will certainly be wrung and possibly be broken. If you want to make sure of keeping it intact, you must give your heart to no one, not even to an animal. Wrap it carefully round with hobbies and little luxuries; avoid all entanglements; lock it up safe in the casket or coffin of your selfishness. But in that casket—safe, dark, motionless, airless—it will change. It will not be broken; it will become unbreakable, impenetrable, irredeemable. . . . The only place outside of Heaven where you can be perfectly safe from all the dangers . . . of love is Hell.[10]

In 2009, Lisa Fenn was an ESPN features television producer looking for a good story. She found it when she met and filmed two young wrestlers at Cleveland's Lincoln-West High School. Seven years later, she wrote about what became a life-changing experience.

Dartanyon Crockett was the high school's top wrestling talent. A winner in multiple weight classes, Dartanyon was also homeless and legally blind. When Lisa met him, he subsisted on the soggy mozzarella sticks and bruised apples served in cafeteria lunches.

Perched atop Dartanyon's back—yes, riding on his back—was wrestling teammate Leroy Sutton. Leroy traveled around up there because he had no legs, and the school had no elevator. When he was eleven, he was hit by a freight train. Paramedics saved his life, but his left leg was amputated below the knee, his right leg below the hip.

Lisa filmed the two boys and their world for five months. Later, editing their story, "Carry On," she "prayed that just one viewer would be moved to help the boys in a meaningful way."

Her prayer was answered. Viewers around the world took the boys into their hearts, and e-mails filled her in-box, offering help.

And that's when love took over. Lisa personally responded to nearly one thousand e-mails. She managed donations, speaking invitations, financial aid forms, and college visits, all while ensuring that Dartanyon and Leroy were finally fed on a daily basis. The generosity of ESPN viewers made it possible for Leroy to move to Arizona to study video game design at Collins College. He became not only the first in his family to graduate from high school, but also the first to receive a college diploma.

The attention brought Dartanyon a different kind of training: In March 2010, coaches invited him to live at the Olympic Training Center in Colorado Springs to learn the Paralympic sport of judo. There he would have shelter, sport, mentors, school, medical care, and, as he proudly showed Lisa on a visit to Colorado, his first bed.

Against the odds, Dartanyon earned a spot on the 2012 Paralympic team going to the London Olympics. And there, he won the bronze. When the medal was draped around Dartanyon's neck, Leroy and Lisa were there to see it.

"Things like this don't happen to kids like us," he cried on that unimaginable night, his face beaming bronze, his tears soaking Lisa's shoulder.

"And he is right," Lisa wrote. "Blind and legless kids from the ghettos don't get college educations and shiny accolades, but they should. And that is why I stayed. Because hope and love and rejoicing and redemption can happen to kids like them."

During a visit to the eye doctor in 2009, Dartanyon included Lisa on the consent form so she could access his records if need be. Later that day, she got a call from the office administrator. "I just thought you should know what Dartanyon wrote on his consent form today," she said. "Next to your name, on the release, is a space that says 'Relationship to Patient.' Dartanyon wrote 'Guardian Angel.'"[11]

Why did Lisa Fenn stay in these boys' lives when she could easily have moved on? She stayed because she loved them.

PRACTICE LOVE EVERY DAY

Just as we learn to walk one step at a time, we learn to love one loving act at a time. We cannot become loving people by doing one gigantic act of love. We learn to love by incorporating love into all of the little things we do. "Let all that you do be done with love" (1 Cor. 16:14).

> We think giving our all to the Lord is like taking a 1,000 dollar bill and laying it on the table—"Here's my life, Lord. I'm giving it all."
>
> But the reality for most of us is that he sends us to the bank and has us cash in the $1,000 for quarters. We go through life putting out 25 cents here, 50 cents there. Listen to the neighbor kid's troubles instead of saying, "Get lost." Go to a committee meeting. Give a cup of water to a shaky old man in a nursing home.
>
> Usually giving our life to Christ isn't glorious. It's done in all those little acts of love, 25 cents at a time.[12]

We'd rather just do one big thing and get it over with—and maybe get a pat on the back in return (more about that in chapter 8 when we discover the life of humility). But as we will see, the life beyond amazing is not flashy. It's lived out in small, everyday ways over the course of a lifetime.

> *Beloved, let us love one another, for love is of God; and everyone who loves is born of God and knows God.*
>
> —1 JOHN 4:7

CHAPTER 2

A LIFE OF JOY

*Joy is the flag that is flown from the castle
of your heart when the King is in residence.*

Gretchen Rubin was living what anyone would call a good life. She had a handsome, loving husband, two adorable daughters, excellent relationships with her family and friends, a successful career, a comfortable home, and good health. Yet despite all this, she often felt angry, melancholy, insecure, listless, guilt-ridden, and unduly upset by minor setbacks.

One rainy day while riding a downtown bus, Gretchen looked out the blurry window and realized she was caught on a treadmill. Life was slipping by, and she wasn't enjoying it. She wasn't depressed, and this wasn't a midlife crisis. It was a feeling of deep discontent that something essential was missing. As she gazed out the water-streaked window, she asked herself, *What do I want from life, anyway?* The answer came back, *Well . . . I want to be happy.*

Gretchen was gripped by fear—a fear that she'd never find happiness. *The days are long, but the years are short*, she thought. *Time is passing, and I'm not focusing enough on things that really matter.* What changes could she make to find the missing pieces to the puzzle? It was something she had to do. She decided to spend a year retooling her life in ways that would lift her out of her malaise and bring on the happiness she was missing.

It's natural for people to struggle with happiness in the face of disappointment or loss, but many of us are like Gretchen Rubin. We're not facing serious difficulty and may even be blessed with love, family, good homes, and good jobs—all things that are supposed to add up to a good life. Yet real happiness eludes us. Life plods on, day after day. Habits settle into routines, and the mere ordinariness of life drags us into a sense of malaise. We experience no real unhappiness, but neither do we experience real joy.

Gretchen Rubin's search for happiness led her to philosophers, noted authors, and popular gurus. She read Plato, Montaigne, Thoreau, Bertrand Russell, Oprah, the Dalai Lama, Buddha, Tolstoy, and Virginia Woolf. Her conclusion was that we can build happiness into our lives through behaviors and attitudes, such as discipline, aiming high, good habits, positive outlook, passion, contemplation, and willed contentment.

Gretchen wrote about her journey in her blockbuster book, *The Happiness Project*. Clearly, she hit a nerve, because her book spent two years on the *New York Times* bestseller list![1]

What is this malaise that affects so many of us? I think it's more than just the absence of happiness. I believe it's the absence of the joy that comes from a deeper relationship with God. The Lord wants us to rejoice in Him, and what God has promised us transcends anything else: God has promised us joy.

Throughout the Bible, the words *happiness* and *joy* are used almost interchangeably. But in Christian practice, when we strive for the fruit of the Spirit, joy imparts a permanent, inner change of heart, mind, and soul. It is well and good and even healthy to strive for happiness, but it's indescribable to experience the joy of the love of Jesus Christ.

THE DIFFERENCE BETWEEN HAPPINESS AND JOY

In the comedy *Cool Runnings*, John Candy plays a former American gold medalist bobsledder who's coaching the first Jamaican bobsled team to go to the Olympics. The bobsledders grow to like the American coach, and eventually Candy's character admits to a dark history. In an Olympics following his gold-medal performance, he added weights to the US sled to make it go downhill faster. He got caught, disgracing himself and his team.

One of the Jamaican bobsledders couldn't understand why anyone who'd already won a gold medal would cheat. He asked John Candy to explain. "I had to win," Candy's character said. "But I learned something. If you're not happy without a gold medal, you won't be happy with one either."[2]

If there's one country on earth where people should be happy, it's the United States of America. But depression affects more than 19 percent of American adults,[3] and anxiety disorders affect more than 40 million, or 18 percent of the population.[4] A 2016 federal data analysis found that suicide rates in America had surged to their highest level in thirty years, rising in that period by 63 percent among middle-aged women and 43 percent among men of that same age.[5]

A worldwide study of 90,000 people showed the ten richest countries in the world also had the highest rates of depression. The United States had the second-highest rate, exceeded only by France.[6] This tells us that joy and happiness aren't dependent on wealth and circumstances. Those who have the most reason to be joyful are often the most depressed.

"We Americans are obsessed with being happy," says theologian and philosopher J. P. Moreland. "But we are also terribly confused about what happiness is. As a result, we seldom find a happiness that lasts. But because 'the pursuit of happiness' is promised to us as a right in the founding document of our nation, the Declaration of Independence, we carry a sense of entitlement. We think we deserve happiness. And if we don't find what we consider to be happiness, we are likely to develop what . . . Alexis de Tocqueville called 'a strange melancholy in the midst of abundance.'"[7]

What an apt description of the attitude of most Americans—surrounded by all the things we think will make us happy, and yet restless and dissatisfied inside. According to one mom,

> what we have is never enough. We always want more. If we're hungry and the food bank is passing out bread, we want two loaves instead of just one. If the church is giving away free coffee after Sunday service, we're irritated that it isn't Starbucks. If we're single, we want to be married. If we're married, we want a better spouse. We want to be thinner, prettier, and richer. We want a good job, then a better one. Then, that job is no longer the best job, so we search for the next job. And we're raising children who are just as bad. They often aren't grateful for the new toy, they want the best toy. They're not sensitive to financial boundaries, because culture (that's us) permeates the greed of more,

more, more. And the pursuit of that façade will never make us happy or fulfilled or thankful.[8]

Maybe you've experienced this dissatisfaction, this "strange melancholy" in your life. Perhaps the pursuit of happiness seems futile, because you're convinced something is always waiting around the bend to snatch away the happiness you've worked so hard to find.

The good news is the joy of a life beyond amazing isn't the same thing as the general happiness that eludes you. Happiness is about what *happens* to you; and, to an extent, it's dependent on your circumstances, your behaviors, and your attitudes. But the joy of Christ is much, much bigger. The joy of Christ is about a relationship with a person. It's something you have access to, but it's also something you must choose.

THE CHRISTIAN LIFE IS INFUSED WITH JOY

The Christian life is marked by notable milestones, and you'll find joy in every one of them. Remember, just because something is important and serious doesn't mean it can't also be filled with joy and the beauty of deep, abiding contentment.

Salvation

The moment of salvation is inexpressibly joyous. This is our eternal, spiritual delivery from separation from God and our entry into the kingdom of God. Jesus came so that we might be saved, and the New Testament testifies that this experience is an occasion for joy—for those converted and for those involved in the process. Many tears of joy have been shed when someone estranged from

God, or who has been an enemy of God, has become His adopted son or daughter.

In Luke 15, Jesus told three stories of precious things that are lost and then found, and each is an occasion for joy: the shepherd who left ninety-nine sheep to search for and find one lost lamb; the woman who lost a valuable coin and found it; and the prodigal son, who was lost but finds his way home. In each story Jesus spoke of the rejoicing that surrounds the saving of one soul, and He described the joy that results: "I say to you that likewise there will be more joy in heaven over one sinner who repents than over ninety-nine just persons who need no repentance" (v. 7).

After the Ethiopian eunuch was saved, he went on his way rejoicing (Acts 8:39). Luke recorded the conversion of the Gentiles "caused great joy to all the brethren" (Acts 15:3). The Philippian jailer and his family were filled with joy when they became believers in God (Acts 16:34). Never doubt that salvation, the most profound of new beginnings, is also infused with joy beyond description.

Baptism

Ask most Christians which is the most joyful event in a church service, and many will say baptism. Joy surrounds baptism.

Years ago, when I was a pastor in Indiana, I became friends with another pastor who told me amazing stories of God's work in his congregation. One Sunday, as he was preaching, a homeless man came into his church and sat down in the front. He listened to the gospel message intently, and at the end of the service, he gave his heart to the Lord.

This church practiced immediate baptism. If you became a Christian, they baptized you that same day at the close of the service. According to my friend, this man was so joyful about his conversion and baptism that he came up out of the water, threw both hands in the air, and shouted, "Hot dog! Hot dog!" He hadn't learned to say, "Amen," "Praise the Lord," or "Hallelujah." All he knew was "Hot dog! Hot dog!" My friend said that was one of the most joyous days he could remember as a pastor.

Trial and Discouragement

Christian joy shows up not only in the happy times but also in times of trial and discouragement. Jesus' joy survived troubles and even flourished in the midst of them. He told His followers: "Blessed are you when men hate you, and when they exclude you, and revile you, and cast out your name as evil, for the Son of Man's sake. Rejoice in that day and leap for joy!" (Luke 6:22–23).

The writers of the epistles followed Jesus' lead:

- "You received the message with joy from the Holy Spirit in spite of the severe suffering it brought you" (1 Thess. 1:6 NLT).
- "My brethren, count it all joy when you fall into various trials" (James 1:2).

One of my favorite Bible stories is the story of Paul and Silas in the Philippian jail. They were beaten; they were imprisoned; and who knew what would happen to them the next day? "But at midnight Paul and Silas were praying and singing hymns to God, and the prisoners were listening to them" (Acts 16:25). The kind of joy that gets you singing in jail at midnight with your back bleeding and your life hanging by a thread—that's joy worth cultivating!

In our culture of instant gratification and constant amusement, it's hard to understand the suffering the apostles endured for the sake of the gospel. We'll do anything to avoid trials and tribulations. But often, in an attempt to keep anything uncomfortable from touching us, we miss the very thing God wants to use to lead us to the joy in Him. We can't avoid difficulties, but in the midst of all our troubles—there is God and His effervescent love.

This doesn't mean we deny or disguise our feelings. It doesn't mean we can or should shrug off pain or disappointment, or try not to feel sorrow when we have good cause. It means we place our trust in God, and He opens the door to a joy beyond anything we can know on our own: the joy of knowing we are in His hands forever.

Commenting on the New Testament's command that we're to rejoice and be glad when undergoing trials, Philip Yancey said:

> By using words like "Rejoice!" the apostles were not advocating a spirit of grin-and-bear-it or act-tough-like-nothing-happened. No trace of those attitudes can be found in Christ's response to suffering, or in Paul's. . . .
>
> Nor is there any masochistic hint of enjoying pain. "Rejoicing in suffering" does not mean that Christians should act happy about tragedy and pain when they feel like crying. Rather, the Bible aims the spotlight on the end result, the productive use God can make of suffering in our lives. To achieve that result, however, he first needs our commitment of trust, and the process of giving him that commitment can be described as rejoicing.[9]

Death

Christian joy is so complete and lasting that it stays with us even when we are dying.

Tony Snow was one of America's most successful and respected newsmen and commentators. He rose from an op-ed writer and editor for a small newspaper to become a voice on ABC's *Good Morning America* and other network shows. His career took off when he moved to Fox News as host of his own show and was a frequent commentator on others. In 2006, President George W. Bush appointed Snow to be his White House press secretary. Though popular, knowledgeable, and highly articulate, he was forced to resign less than two years later when he was diagnosed with terminal colon cancer. He died the following year at fifty-three.

Tony Snow could have died a bitter man, angry at how his brilliant career was cut short at its peak and how cancer deprived him of life with his wife and three children. But Tony was a devout Christian. Far from being angry at God, he found joy in the unexpected blessing his illness brought him. He communicated this joy eloquently in an article published a few months before his death.

God relishes surprise. We want lives of simple, predictable ease—smooth, even trails as far as the eye can see—but God likes to go off-road. He provokes us with twists and turns. He places us in predicaments that seem to defy our endurance and comprehension—and yet don't. By his love and grace, we persevere. The challenges that make our hearts leap and stomachs churn invariably strengthen our faith and grant measures of wisdom and joy we would not experience otherwise. . . .

The mere thought of death somehow makes every blessing vivid, every happiness more luminous and intense. We may not know how our contest with sickness will end, but we have felt the ineluctable touch of God.[10]

As Paul contemplated the conclusion of his life and ministry, he anticipated the joy that would be his at the end: "But none of these things move me; nor do I count my life dear to myself, so that I may finish my race with joy" (Acts 20:24). According to the apostle Peter, this joy is "inexpressible" (1 Peter 1:8). From his captivity on the Isle of Patmos, John the apostle affirmed this dying joy: "Blessed are the dead who die in the Lord" (Rev. 14:13).

G. K. Chesterton believed this joy is "the gigantic secret of the Christian."[11] And I believe he's right. Joy that thrives from the moment of our salvation to the moment of our death cannot be found outside of Christ! And what God desires for us, He also provides for us. Let's look at the keys to true and lasting joy—a joy that will lift you out of dullness and malaise and raise you far above the direst of conditions and worst of circumstances.

GOD WANTS YOU TO BE JOYFUL

Author Bruce Larson wrote:

> "Joy is the surest sign of the presence of God." . . . The bottom line for you and me is simply this: grimness is not a Christian virtue. There are no sad saints. If God really is the center of one's life and being, joy is inevitable. If we have no joy, we have missed the heart of the Good News and our bodies as much as our souls will suffer the consequences.[12]

God experiences joy; and if we're His, we'll experience it too. In fact, God's greatest joys seem to be about His people!

- "As the bridegroom rejoices over the bride, so shall your God rejoice over you" (Isa. 62:5).

- "I will rejoice in Jerusalem, and joy in My people" (Isa. 65:19).

When we're in a right relationship with God, He rejoices. And it's only through that relationship that we experience joy in its fullness.

Jesus was completely comfortable at joyous events. In fact, the first miracle of Jesus took place at a wedding celebration. It was performed in a setting of rejoicing, not a setting of mourning; it was a wedding, not a wake or funeral.

Throughout the New Testament, the Lord generously imparted His joy to others. One day He healed a crippled woman. She stood straight up and began praising the Lord (Luke 13:13). The Samaritan leper healed by Jesus returned to thank him, "praising God in a loud voice" (Luke 17:15 NIV). When the lame man at the Beautiful Gate was healed, he got up and went into the temple, "walking, leaping, and praising God" (Acts 3:8).[13]

Describing these moments in the life of Jesus, Paul wrote: "For the kingdom of God is . . . righteousness and peace and joy in the Holy Spirit" (Rom. 14:17). Many Christians have the righteousness part down and maybe even the peace part. But they're clueless when it comes to joy. Instead of enjoying the Christian life, they seem to endure it.

In the Bible, we're told to "rejoice with those who rejoice, and weep with those who weep" (Rom. 12:15). I know many sincere Christians who are good at weeping and not so good at rejoicing. Yet, as Lewis Smedes wrote: "You and I were created for joy, and if we miss it, we miss the reason for our existence."[14]

Jesus made it very clear that our joy is a priority for Him when He said, "These things I have spoken to you, that My joy may remain in you, and that your joy may be full" (John 15:11).

God not only desires for us to be joyful; He actually *commands* it: "Rejoice in the Lord always. Again I will say, rejoice!" (Phil. 4:4).

Perhaps you're thinking that you can't just tell someone to be happy. How can anyone command joy? Rob Morgan shares the answer:

> We may not be able to rejoice in our load, but we can rejoice in our Lord. We may find no joy in our situation, but we can rejoice in our Savior. To rejoice in the Lord means we rejoice in our unassailable, unchanging relationship with the sovereign Lord and in His qualities, gifts, promises, and attributes.[15]

I speak for many who are Christ-followers: we *must* get better at living life joyously. Jesus experienced and expressed joy in life, and so should we. When I wake up in the morning, I often repeat these words of the psalmist, taking liberty to replace *we* with *I*: "This is the day the Lord has made; [I] will rejoice and be glad in it" (Ps. 118:24).

Try it. Write down this verse, and keep it by your bed so it's the first thing you see in the morning. Say it aloud or in your heart to yourself and to God. Trust me. This one small act will begin opening your heart to joy.

SURRENDER TO JESUS CHRIST

At the *center* of the joy that God promises is Jesus Christ Himself. Christian joy is letting Christ live out His life through you so that what He *is* you *become*. In Christ we are "strengthened with all might, according to His glorious power, for all patience and longsuffering with joy" (Col. 1:11).

Jesus' joy is also a *complete* joy. It's not an "almost" joy or a "sometimes" joy. It's 100 percent joy! The uniqueness of this joy is captured in Peter's words in the first chapter of his first letter. Peter wrote that even though we've never seen or touched Jesus in the flesh, when we believe in Him, we possess an inexpressible joy, full of glory (1 Peter 1:8).

I remember hearing a story about a headmaster at a boarding school in London. One of his students once remarked that he thought the headmaster went to heaven every night because every morning when he saw him, he had such a wonderful smile on his face. That student figured the only place you could get that kind of joy was by checking in to heaven at the end of every day.

One day the headmaster was asked why he was so filled with joy, and his response was truly a life-beyond-amazing statement: "Joy is the flag that is flown from the castle of your heart when the King is in residence."

In other words, joy is determined by whether or not Jesus Christ is at home in your life.

Have you discovered how easy it is for your gladness of today to become your sadness of tomorrow? For your sweetness of the morning to turn into the bitterness of the night? Have you discovered how people you thought were your friends today can become your enemies tomorrow? And the wisdom you thought was so great yesterday seems foolish today?

Against that backdrop stands our immutable, unchanging Lord. Since our joy is in Jesus and Jesus never changes, the joy of Jesus never changes either. Christian joy is *continuous*, never-ending, constant joy. It is not hinged on happenings; it is perfected in a person.

In the midst of the disciples' sorrow and anxiety as they processed the words of His impending death and departure from them, Jesus comforted them, saying: "Therefore you now have sorrow; but I will see you again and your heart will rejoice, and your joy no one will take from you" (John 16:22).

We can take great courage in this truth. Joy isn't an emotion that comes and goes; it's an attitude that comes and grows. How does this joy become a part of our lives? What do we need to do to experience it? Surrender to Christ.

Joy comes when Christ comes to live within your heart. We can't have the joy of Christ until we have the Christ of joy: "And my soul shall be joyful in the LORD; it shall rejoice in His salvation" (Ps. 35:9).

C. S. Lewis described this joy sixty-five years ago in terms that make just as much sense today:

> A car is made to run on petrol, and it would not run properly on anything else. Now God designed the human machine to run on Himself. He Himself is the fuel our spirits were designed to burn, or the food our spirits were designed to feed on. There is no other. That is why it is just no good asking God to make us happy in our own way without bothering about religion. God cannot give us a happiness and peace apart from Himself, because it is not there. There is no such thing.[16]

Some of you may not know Christian joy because you've never put your trust in the Lord Jesus Christ. Let me encourage you in the words of a song we sang in church when I was growing up: "If you want joy, real joy, wonderful joy, let Jesus come into your heart."

SUBMIT TO THE SPIRIT OF GOD

The Holy Spirit is the purveyor of joy. When you become a Christian, the Holy Spirit comes to live within you. He becomes ever present in your life. This is part of the gift of salvation—the indwelling of the Holy Spirit. Throughout your life, you get to decide whether to turn your life over to His guidance. When you decide to give Him control of your life, He will bring His joy to you.

Perhaps one reason you're not experiencing the joy of the Lord is that you haven't given control of your life to the Holy Spirit who lives within you. As I often tell my congregation, the Holy Spirit does not want to be a *resident* in your life; He wants to be the *President* of your life.

Most of us go through life trying to figure out who we report to, who we're responsible to. It's a constant state of indecision and confusion. But when we give ourselves to the Holy Spirit, we eliminate that confusion. We open ourselves to His guidance, and in doing so, we feel the quiet joy of knowing that all will be well.

The Holy Spirit guides us in our quest to achieve the fruit of the Spirit, and we'll have much more to say about Him later. For now, remember that the Holy Spirit wants us to be joyful. I promise you, joy and the Holy Spirit go together.

- "For the kingdom of God is not eating and drinking, but righteousness and peace and joy in the Holy Spirit" (Rom. 14:17).
- "And you became followers of us and of the Lord, having received the word in much affliction, with joy of the Holy Spirit" (1 Thess. 1:6).

STUDY THE WORD OF GOD

The Bible is God's handbook on joy, so take time to read it. The New King James translation of the Bible contains more than four hundred references to *joy, joyful, joyfully, joyous, rejoice,* and *rejoicing*. No matter where you begin reading the Bible, you'll bump into joy before you read very far.

If I were looking for the best place to start studying joy in the Bible, I'd start with Paul's letter to the Philippians. The theme of this letter is joy; the word *rejoice* is found nine times and the word *joy* four times. Even though he was writing *as a prisoner,* Paul was filled with joy, and that joy permeates his letter.

What was the source of Paul's joy? It was his relationship with Jesus Christ. Philippians begins and ends with the name of Jesus, and Paul mentions Jesus Christ forty times in the four short chapters of his letter.

One of the prime results of reading Scripture is the cultivation of joy in our hearts, and one of the best illustrations of the relationship between teaching God's Word and joy is found in the Old Testament book of Ezra.

On a particular day Ezra gathered the people of Israel together for the purpose of teaching them the Word of God. The congregation stood during the entire sermon (Neh. 8:5).

"So they read distinctly from the book, in the Law of God; and they gave the sense, and helped them to understand the reading" (v. 8). And just a few verses later we read, "And all the people went their way to eat and drink . . . and rejoice greatly, because they understood the words that were declared to them" (v. 12).

I love to watch the people of God as they come to church each week. I can usually identify those who are hungry for the Word of God. There's an attitude of expectation on their faces. When I teach God's Word, their joy comes alive.

The Word of God is what the Spirit of God uses to guide our lives. And if we don't cooperate with the Holy Spirit by reading and studying God's Word, He doesn't have anything to work with. Joy results from understanding the Word of God.

The prophet Jeremiah beautifully describes the joy he derived from the Word of God: "Your words were found, and I ate them, and Your word was to me the joy and rejoicing of my heart" (Jer. 15:16).

SPEND TIME IN PRAYER

Jesus said, "Until now you have asked nothing in My name. Ask, and you will receive, that your joy may be full" (John 16:24). Did you know that you can come to God in prayer and ask Him to fill you with joy?

That's what the psalmist was doing in Psalm 86:4 when he said, "Rejoice the soul of Your servant, for to You, O Lord, I lift up my soul."

When we are troubled, praying for joy can feel like the last thing we can bring ourselves to do. We want to pray for relief from our disappointment, sorrow, or fear. We want to pray for our pain or anxiety to be lifted from us. Praying for joy seems way down on our list of things for which to ask.

I understand. But remember, joy doesn't have to be what we think of as rejoicing. It can also be quiet joy, the comforting joy of knowing that you belong to God through Jesus Christ. It can be the reassuring and uplifting joy of knowing that you are never alone; God is always with you.

Here's how one author prayed Psalm 86:4, when his soul was struggling to find joy:

> God, I lift up to you my dry, languishing soul. I turn to you because I believe you can restore its joy. I want you alone. I want you to fill me, to fill my soul—to fill my whole being—with joy. Where else can I turn, if not to you? To you alone I lift up my soul, for in you alone will I find the true gladness my soul longs for.[17]

During a break at a Christian women's conference, Joni Eareckson Tada was asked about her joy. In the article "Joy Hard Won," Joni said the women wanted to know how she could look so happy in her wheelchair:

> "I don't do it," I said. "In fact, may I tell you honestly how I woke up this morning?
>
> "This is an average day," I breathed deeply. "After my husband, Ken, leaves for work at 6:00 a.m., I'm alone until I hear the front door open at 7:00 a.m. That's when a friend arrives to get me up.
>
> "While I listen to her make coffee, I pray, 'Oh, Lord, my friend will soon give me a bath, get me dressed, sit me up in my chair, brush my hair and teeth, and send me out the door. I don't have the strength to face this routine one more time. I have no resources. I don't have a smile to take into the day. But you do. May I have yours? God, I need you desperately.'"
>
> "So, what happens when your friend comes through the bedroom door?" one of them asked.
>
> "I turn my head toward her and give her a smile sent straight from heaven. It's not mine. It's God's. And so," I said, gesturing to my paralyzed legs, "whatever joy you see today was hard won this morning."[18]

SHARE YOUR LIFE WITH OTHERS

Being a Christian isn't always easy, and we make it much harder on ourselves when we try to do it alone. This is one reason Christians have such a heart for those on the mission field or those in prison; they may not have others with whom they can share their joy in Jesus Christ.

To truly share your joy in being a Christian requires more than mere church attendance. It means immersing yourself in the life of the church and forming active relationships with authentic Christians. How do you find authentic Christians? They will be the joyful ones. They will display an easy, friendly confidence. They will be interested in others and care for each other.

Periodically over the years, people who have attended our church have written me notes complaining about the members behaving irreverently when they enter the worship center prior to the services. These notes are in reference to the greeting, visiting, chatter, and laughter that, according to the writer of the note, destroys the somber atmosphere required for authentic worship.

I want to humbly disagree with this. This chatter and laughter is the joyful noise of connection and relationship that binds our church together. It is the best sound a church can hear as a prelude to its worship of God.

In the words of scholar William Barclay, "the Christian is the man of joy. The Christian is the laughing cavalier of Christ. A gloomy Christian is a contradiction in terms, and nothing in all religious history has done Christianity more harm than its black clothes and long faces."[19]

Christian joy is contagious, and to catch it you must expose yourself to the virus and become part of the blessed epidemic!

In his autobiography, *Just as I Am*, Billy Graham tells about being invited for lunch at the home of one of the world's wealthiest men on an island in the Caribbean. Throughout lunch, the seventy-five-year-old man seemed close to tears, finally saying, "I am the most miserable man in the world. Out there is my yacht. I can go anywhere I want. I have my private plane, my helicopters. I have everything I want to make my life happy, yet I am miserable as hell."

The Grahams talked and prayed with the man, doing their best to point him to Christ, who alone would be able to give him the deep meaning in life he sought.

After leaving the man's beautiful home, the Grahams returned to the small cottage where they were staying on the island. That afternoon the pastor of the local Baptist church came to call. In spite of his limited resources and difficult situation, he was full of enthusiasm and love for Christ. "I don't have two pounds to my name," he said with a smile, "but I am the happiest man on this island."

After the pastor left, Billy Graham turned to his wife and asked, "Who do you think is the richer man?"

Ruth Graham didn't even need to reply, for the answer was obvious.

What the rich man was seeking was happiness—a reason to laugh and forget his troubles. What the pastor had already found was a deep-seated joy based not on what he possessed, but on who possessed him—Jesus Christ.[20]

The joy of the LORD is your strength.

—NEHEMIAH 8:10

CHAPTER 3

A LIFE OF PEACE

Peace is not the absence of stress
but the presence of the Savior.

As I was writing this chapter, my wife and I were staying at the Marriott Marquis Hotel in New York City. That day, May 18, 2017, an intoxicated man drove his car over the curb, killing an eighteen-year-old girl and injuring twenty-two others. His car finally stopped when it smashed into the barriers in front of our hotel.

I'd come to New York to speak to a group of pastors, part of an event sponsored by one of the networks that carries our radio program. The pastor's event was in Brooklyn, more than an hour's drive in traffic from our hotel. Since I was going to be involved all morning, I'd encouraged Donna to stay at our hotel, get up a bit later, and enjoy a relaxing morning.

As our event in Brooklyn was ending, I was told there'd been an incident in Manhattan. At that point many assumed it was an act of terrorism. My heart raced as I tried to call Donna. At first we couldn't connect, but minutes later I was relieved to hear her voice. She told me she was okay but the hotel was locked down. If you saw television coverage of that incident, you were probably as shocked as I was to see Times Square completely empty.

My heart went out to the injured and their families, and my focus moved to how to get to the hotel to pick up my wife so we could go home. But all streets leading to Times Square were cordoned off. As I was trying to figure out what to do, I got a call from the guest manager of the hotel, who is also our friend. He told me not to worry; he would handle things. Within a few minutes, he directed our driver to an intersection two blocks from the hotel. The hotel manager had talked to the chief of police, and he told us to ask for a particular lieutenant when we got to this intersection. That officer, he said, would let us through the barricades so we could get to the hotel.

Sure enough, we arrived at the appointed intersection and met the lieutenant and two of his officers. The chief of police had wired them a picture of me that I think came from Wikipedia. They scrutinized the picture, then looked carefully at me, finally deciding we were one and the same.

Then, to my total surprise, all three of them came over to the car with their printouts of my photo. They told me how much they loved our television program and thanked us for caring about New York City. They asked me to autograph their pictures. Then they removed the barricades and let our car through. My God is an awesome God, and He is full of surprises!

I am telling you this story because for a few minutes that morning I felt fear grip my heart. In that moment, I did not feel peace.

My thoughts were on my wife and the terrible incident in front of our hotel. What if Donna had decided to take a walk in front of our hotel that morning? (She told me later she'd actually considered doing that.) What if I couldn't reach her? What if . . . ?

In the face of uncertainty, tragedy, and danger, we all have moments when we're overcome, when we lose sight of the peace our Lord brought us. In these times our work—and it's not always easy—is to turn our thoughts and hearts back to God's peace, the peace that passes all understanding. Our work is to immerse ourselves in the peace of Jesus Christ.

THE WORLD YEARNS FOR PEACE

Inching our way through traffic on the way back to the hotel, it was sobering to realize how many people in our world live under this kind of threat every day of their lives.

In an article she wrote for *Christianity Today,* Sarah Lebhar Hall tells about her struggle with peace:

> I was in Atlanta for a conference. While there, I heard news of a possible ISIS threat against the city. The FBI, I was told, was taking the threat seriously, and we were to remain alert. While the credibility of the threat was unclear, I have to admit I felt anxious as I went to bed that night. I was far from my family. My young children were counting down the days until they would see me again. Warding off fear, I turned to read Isaiah 9.
>
> I was comforted by this reminder that God hates terror more than we do. He's not satisfied with people living in the constant shadow of death. He has a plan for permanently eradicating the

things that terrify us—the sound of stamping boots, scary news reports, red alert levels at the airport, horrifying Internet videos. Brutal regimes will make their plans, but God can out-strategize them all. His plan for his children is over-the-top joy. No more oppression. No more spilled blood. And while we have seen this plan put into action in the giving of Jesus, it is not yet complete. It's still expanding, and it has a long way to go. But we know this: God is passionately committed to rescuing us from the specter of death.[1]

PEACE: GOD'S ULTIMATE GOAL

God's ultimate goal for humanity is for peace to blanket the earth. His Son, Jesus Christ, was called the "Prince of Peace" by Isaiah the prophet (Isa. 9:6). That's because Isaiah saw another day on the prophetic horizon. He described that day as a time when nations would "beat their swords into plowshares, and their spears into pruning hooks; nation shall not lift up sword against nation, neither shall they learn war anymore" (2:4).

So universal is the longing for peace that this verse, Isaiah 2:4, is engraved on the Isaiah Wall in a park across the street from the United Nations building in New York City.

Our yearning for peace is expressed around the world in enormous statues and works of art. If our Statue of Liberty means anything, it means we are offering a gesture of peace to those who come to live within this country. It's a symbol of our desire for peace in the world. Christ of the Andes, on the border between Chile and Argentina, is a gigantic figure constructed to celebrate and express the hope for peace. In Paris, there's the Wall for Peace at the foot of the Eiffel Tower. This glass monument has the word *peace* written in forty-nine languages, and visitors are encouraged to leave messages of peace in the cracks. In Tokyo stands a robust statue with arms outstretched toward heaven, and written underneath the statue in Greek and Japanese is the word *agape* . . . a testimony to the desire of the Japanese people for peace between their country and others.

Many years ago a man from the Dominican Republic was so concerned and burdened about world peace that he offered himself to be nailed to a cross as a sacrifice for world peace. As thousands watched on television, six-inch stainless steel spikes were driven into his hands and feet. He had planned to remain on the cross for forty-eight hours, but after only twenty hours he had to cut short his voluntary crucifixion because of an infection that developed in his right foot. The newspaper headline the next day read as follows: "Crucifixion for Peace Falls Short."[2]

That headline could summarize just about everything that's been done in our world to find true peace. It all has fallen short of its goal. Someone observed that Washington, DC, has a large assortment of peace monuments; we build one after each war.

I may be realistic about the world's efforts to achieve peace, but I am not cynical. Working for peace is a noble effort, perhaps the noblest. Jesus said peacemakers "shall be called sons of God" (Matt. 5:9). And the apostle Paul said, "If it is possible, as much as depends on you, live peaceably with all men" (Rom. 12:18).

Yet as much as everyone claims to want peace in the world, it's been an elusive goal throughout human history. And now we see the world becoming an even more dangerous place. In the midst of all that worries us, how do we find the peace of God?

We make it our mission, and we do the work to receive it.

Think about what you do when you have to be somewhere but you can't find your car keys. You frantically search for them. And while you're searching, you're worrying about where you're supposed to be and who's waiting for you and what you'll miss. You're distracted, upset, and you have no memory of where you left those keys!

But as soon as you find them, the memory of putting them there comes back to you—because it was there all along. You just let other thoughts crowd it out.

God's peace is one of the keys to a life beyond amazing, and finding it is a serious endeavor. Let the desire to know that peace fill your heart and be your focus. Search the likely places and do the likely things with calmness and faith. Don't let the pressure and uncertainty of the world distract you.

Peace is the reason God sent His only Son to earth. He is in truth the Prince of Peace, and His peace is "the peace of God, which surpasses all understanding" (Phil. 4:7). When He appeared for the first time on this earth in a manger in Bethlehem, the angels announced His arrival with these words: "Glory to God in the highest, and on earth peace, goodwill toward men!" (Luke 2:14).

I encourage you to cultivate God's peace in your life. And I can tell you how. First, understand what God's peace means for you. Then, ask for it and desire it with all your heart. Finally, do the things that open your heart to accept it when it arrives.

UNDERSTAND GOD'S PEACE?

The world into which Jesus was born had a very different understanding of the concept of peace than we have today. Our English word *peace* originates from an Old French word meaning "reconciliation, silence, agreement, the absence of hostility."

But the Hebrew word *shalom* has a much richer meaning. This word is found more than two hundred times in the Old Testament. Its basic meaning is "to be whole, or safe, or sound." Shalom designates a condition in which life can best be lived. It is the concept of integrity; body, soul, and spirit are in alignment. In shalom, you have more than the absence of hostility. You have a quality of life that nurtures peace.

Shalom is "the condition of everything being set right. It's about fulfillment, completion, maturity, soundness, wholeness, harmony, tranquility, security, well-being, welfare, friendship, agreement, success, prosperity. It's about the total well-being of the person and the community. It's one of the deepest longings of the human heart."[3]

Shalom means all is well in my life; everything is integrated in my life.

When Jesus came, he brought that certainty to us. He is the only way to have that peace in your life.

Commenting on this peace with God, Ray Stedman wrote with excitement, "Our hearts are at peace! . . . Calmness, courage! To use a modern term, and, I think the most accurate, we have good 'morale.' Our morale is high. We are ready for anything. No ground can be too rough for Christ—and we have Christ. Therefore we have good morale."[4]

About twenty-two years ago I was diagnosed with lymphoma, a type of cancer that, at the time, had a very poor survival rate. Shortly after my diagnosis I went to the Mayo Clinic and was operated on immediately. To determine the extent of the cancer, they basically cut me stem to stern.

After my surgery I was taken to another floor to recover. On this floor the patient rooms were in a circle, with the nurses' station and desks for staff in the middle. As soon as it was possible, the doctors wanted me up and moving around. Of course, that was the last thing I felt like doing. But knowing this was an important part of my recovery, I pushed myself to do a full lap around the nurses' station, starting at my room and passing every other patient's room until I reached my own room again. My goal that first day was one lap, and I was barely able to finish it.

The next day I decided to push myself to do two laps. My plan was to do one more lap each day than I'd done the day before. So I set out, walking slowly around the circle.

By a strange coincidence, the doctor who had performed my surgery was dictating his notes about me when I shuffled by his desk. All I remember hearing him say was, "A pastor who has stage four large cell lymphoma cancer."

Stage 4. I was stunned. Until that moment I hadn't known how serious my condition was. Somehow I completed those two laps and got back to my room. I can remember sitting there, feeling scared and overwhelmed. But then, that feeling completely left me and was replaced by another.

I'm not in control of my life, I told myself. *But the Spirit of God is.*

A sense of what I can only describe as "good morale" came over me. I would let God do His work, and I would do mine. After that, my only thought was, *Well, I'll have to do three laps tomorrow.*

For twenty-two years I didn't share that story with anyone, not even my wife. But as I was writing this chapter, it came powerfully to mind. This resiliently good morale is the peace God gives us when we turn our lives over to Him. In the face of a terrible diagnosis, the Lord's peace was resilient, and I persevered with good morale.

Over the next few months I underwent two rounds of chemotherapy and a stem cell transplant, at the end of which I was in remission. Today I remain cancer-free.

If things are bad on the outside but the Holy Spirit is in charge on the inside, He will give you peace when you surrender your life to Jesus, our Prince of Peace, and express the yearning for His peace in your heart, just as nations express it in monuments. And if you feel discouraged, hold fast to this: real peace is possible. Of that the Bible assures us.

PEACE *WITH* GOD

Paul wrote: "Therefore, having been justified by faith, we have peace with God through our Lord Jesus Christ" (Rom. 5:1). Peace in this passage means the cessation of hostility, not mere tranquility of mind. It's not that we've ceased to be hostile to God, but that God has ceased to be righteously hostile to us as sinners. Sin broke the relationship between God and man: "Your iniquities have separated you from your God" (Isa. 59:2).

The peace Jesus brings changes the image of God from a fisted hand with a gavel to the outstretched hand of a friend. God's anger at us because of our sin is put away. Our separation from Him is overcome. God adopts us into His family. And from now on all His dealings with us are for our good. He will never be against us. He is our Father and our friend. We don't need to be afraid anymore.

In the Greek language the word for peace means "to join together." It pictures two opposing forces that have been separated now being reconciled. And that's what our peace in Jesus Christ is all about. We who were at enmity with God have been brought together by Jesus Christ. He is our peace.

- "For He Himself is our peace, who has made both one, and has broken down the middle wall of separation" (Eph. 2:14).
- "And you, who once were alienated and enemies in your mind by wicked works, yet now He has reconciled in the body of His flesh through death, to present you holy, and blameless, and above reproach in His sight" (Col. 1:21–22).

I see this peace illustrated so beautifully by the cross itself. It points up toward heaven, picturing the fact that Jesus Christ, who was the Son of God, reached up and took hold of the hand of the Father. At the same time, the cross points down toward earth, picturing the fact that Jesus Christ, who was the Son of Man, reached down and took hold of the hands of fallen human beings. And with one hand in the hand of God and the other hand in the hand of man, He brought the two together and made peace.

PEACE *FROM* GOD

Jesus said, "Peace I leave with you, My peace I give to you; not as the world gives do I give to you. Let not your heart be troubled, neither let it be afraid" (John 14:27). Jesus spoke these words on the verge of His own violent execution. It was in the context of a stormy, difficult, unbelievable situation in His life.

Anyone can have peace when things are going well. When all is well at home, when physical health is robust, when finances are manageable, when children are halfway behaving. But it is no credit to us when we have peace in those circumstances because even the world has a semblance of peace in circumstances like that. But when we can have peace in the midst of difficult times, that is the testimony God wants us to bear to this world.

And this peace is not a quiet tension. Quiet tension is not peace. It's just compressed anxiety. Too often we think we're trusting when we're really only controlling our panic. True peace is not only a calm exterior, but also a quiet heart.

There's a wonderful moment the apostle John recorded that brings together this truth about the peace we now have with God. Jesus is making his first postresurrection appearance to His gathered disciples. They are terrified.

> Then, the same day at evening, being the first day of the week, when the doors were shut where the disciples were assembled, for fear of the Jews, Jesus came and stood in the midst, and said to them, "Peace be with you." When He had said this, He showed them His hands and His side. (John 20:19–20)

Jesus was showing them His hands and His side for the purpose of identifying Himself to them. But I believe He was also saying, "These wounds are *why* I can say to you, 'Peace be with you.' For this is how much I loved you; this is what I did to broker peace for your life. I died, and you don't have to be afraid anymore. The deed is done, the victory is won, peace be to you."

It's because of what Jesus did on the cross that we can have this peace. God sent Jesus to be the bridge we can cross to the peace that passes all understanding.

PEACE *OF* GOD

"The peace of God, which surpasses all understanding, will guard your hearts and minds through Christ Jesus" (Phil. 4:7). When the apostle wrote those words, he was a prisoner in Rome. In a cold and lightless dungeon, Paul relied on the peace of God to help him survive. He spoke of an inner calm, a serenity of soul, an inward peace born of faith and trust in God.

Do you enjoy that kind of peace? Are you able to have that inner calmness, that quiet assurance that all is well even though the outward circumstances may be chaotic? Are you able to sleep at night? "I will both lie down in peace, and sleep; for You alone, O LORD, make me dwell in safety" (Ps. 4:8).

No matter what goes on during the day, no matter what the problems are, no matter what frustrations you have at work, or in school, or with the other members of your family, can you feel peace at the end of the day—or even in the midst of it all? While everything is going crazy out there, is there that quiet center in your life that keeps you going in the right direction?

The peace of God acts as a guard at the door of your heart and mind to provide security against the assaults of guilt, worries, threats, confusions, uncertainties—all those things that threaten our peace. God guards our hearts and minds in a way that goes beyond what human understanding can fathom— "which surpasses all understanding." Don't limit the peace of God by what you can see. He gives us inexplicable peace, unimaginable peace.

Philippians 4:9 tells us that not only will we have the peace of God guarding our hearts from the outside, but even better, we will have the God of Peace protecting our hearts from the inside. He will be in us, and His presence will be our comfort and encouragement when difficult problems assail our minds.

There are four main highways upon which the peace of God travels: the Spirit of God, the Son of God, the Word of God, and prayer.

PEACE AND THE SPIRIT OF GOD

When Jesus was teaching His disciples that He had to leave them, He told them about the Holy Spirit and that the Holy Spirit would come to help them—to help you and me. When Jesus was finished with all of His instruction about the Holy Spirit, He said, "These things I have spoken to you, that in Me you may have peace" (John 16:33).

Essentially, Jesus was saying, "I have taught you about the Holy Spirit, and I want you to know about Him because if you know about the Holy Spirit and you understand how He works in your life, then you can have peace. He is the Spirit of peace." And that's why the fruit of the Spirit includes peace.

Peace is the inevitable result of the Spirit of God controlling your life. How can you tell if you are controlled by the Spirit of God? By the quietness within you when difficulty, pain, and turmoil surround you.

In 2012, Kara and Jason Tippetts and their four beautiful children moved to Colorado Springs to begin the adventure of a lifetime. They were going to start a church. During this time, Kara decided to start a simple mommy blog, *Mundane Faithfulness*, dedicated to chronicling her family's journey and helping other moms parent with kindness. But in the summer of that year, she was diagnosed with breast cancer, and *Mundane Faithfulness* was transformed "into a place where Kara processed her diagnosis and treatment, and where she articulated her heart in response to her pain."[5]

Soon her following grew as she wrote about the grace and peace she was finding in her suffering. A publisher discovered her blog, and in the fall of 2014, her first book, *The Hardest Peace*, was released followed by two more in the subsequent years.

Just over a year later, on March 22, 2015, Kara won her battle with cancer and went home to Jesus. But her blog and books continue to be an inspiration and encouragement to thousands around the world. Near the end of her life, she wrote:

> My little body has grown tired of battle, and treatment is no longer helping. But what I see, what I know, what I have is Jesus. He has still given me breath, and with it I pray I would live well and fade well. By degrees doing both, living and dying, as I have moments left to live. I get to draw my people close, kiss them and tenderly speak love over their lives. I get to pray into eternity my hopes and fears for the moments of my loves. I get to laugh and cry and wonder over Heaven. I do not feel like I have the courage for this journey, but I have Jesus—and He will provide. He has given me so much to be grateful for, and that gratitude, that wondering over His love, will cover us all. And it will carry us—carry us in ways we cannot comprehend.[6]

In the hardest days of her life, Kara Tippetts was marked by an amazing sense of gratitude and love. She was carried by a peace beyond comprehension, a peace only the Holy Spirit can provide.

PEACE AND THE SON OF GOD

I once saw a church billboard that said it all:

> *No Christ, No peace.*
> *Know Christ, Know Peace.*

When Jesus was preparing His disciples for His departure from them, He encouraged them with these words: "Let not your heart be troubled; you believe in God, believe also in Me. . . . Peace I leave with you, My peace I give to you; not as the world gives do I give to you. Let not your heart be troubled, neither let it be afraid" (John 14:1, 27).

A few verses later, Jesus expanded on His earlier promise: "These things I have spoken to you, that in Me you may have peace. In the world you will have tribulation; but be of good cheer, I have overcome the world" (John 16:33).

During the blitz in London in World War II, when German bombs were raining down on the city, the people lived in constant fear. It's hard for us to imagine the kind of deep, pervasive anxiety—even terror—that results from continual bombardment. During those dark days, one man's undaunted voice would regularly ring out from radios all over the nation, inspiring them to new hope and new belief. Their cause was just; their government was resolute; their armies would not fail them. The people listened and took heart.

What Winston Churchill did for the English during World War II, Jesus Christ does for us. Today conflicts abound in the world, and as I write this there are cities under bombardment in the Middle East. Yet He comes to us in the midst of the struggle, when the battle is almost unbearable and the circumstances look impossible. In the voice of absolute certainty, of power and strength beyond imagining, He speaks to us of peace and gives us the encouragement we need. He raises our morale and fills us with the deep strength that peace imparts so we can go back into the battle to quell the fear with God's peace and be victorious.[7]

In *Deserted by God?* Sinclair Ferguson told the following story:

The first physician to die of the AIDS virus in the United Kingdom was a young Christian. He had contracted it while doing medical research in Bulawayo, Zimbabwe. In the last days of his life, his power of communication failed. He struggled with increasing difficulty to express his thoughts to his wife. On one occasion she simply could not understand his message. He wrote on a note pad the letter J. She ran through her medical dictionary, saying various words beginning with J. None was right. Then she said, "Jesus?"

That was the right word. He was with them. That was all either of them needed to know. That is always enough.[8]

One of the best verses on peace in the Bible is from the book of Isaiah: "You will keep him in perfect peace, whose mind is stayed on You" (Isa. 26:3).

Henri Nouwen wrote:

Keep your eyes on the prince of peace, the one who doesn't cling to his divine power; the one who refuses to turn stones into bread, jump from great heights, and rule with great power; the one who touches the lame, the crippled, and the blind; the one who speaks words of forgiveness and encouragement. Keep your eyes on him who becomes poor with the poor, weak with the weak. He is the source of all peace.[9]

When we keep our eyes and minds focused on the reality of Christ rather than the inevitable problems of this life, we are spiritually and mentally invincible. I love this question that is tucked away in the book of Job: "When He gives quietness, who then can make trouble?" (Job 34:29). Here is my prayer for all of us, borrowed from the prayer Paul prayed for his friends in Thessalonica: "Now may the Lord of peace Himself give you peace always in every way" (2 Thess. 3:16).

PEACE AND THE WORD OF GOD

The psalmist used all but two of the 176 verses of Psalm 119, the longest chapter in the Bible, to extol the virtues of the Word of God. When he was just eleven verses from the end of that psalm, he filed this report: "Great peace have those who love Your law, and nothing causes them to stumble" (v. 165).

Of the twenty-seven New Testament books, eighteen begin with a greeting of peace. And this peace was not just from the human authors of each letter, from Paul, Peter, or John. No, this greeting of peace is from God the Father and the Lord Jesus Christ! In every instance, it's grace and then peace, not the other way around.

This is because there's no peace unless God extends His grace to us. Until you experience the grace of God, you can't have peace. This is so basic to the understanding of the early Christians that it is the official greeting Paul used to introduce himself: "Grace and peace to you."

You'd think it might be reversed at least once, right? But it isn't. It's grace first, then peace. And its prevalence in the Bible reminds us that this is, indeed, how it has to work; without grace, there is no peace!

Did you know the word *peace* occurs nearly four hundred times in the Bible, not to mention many other verses about strength, security, and comfort? The Bible is the Word of the God of peace, and it's full of peace. Memorizing some of these truths is like installing a personal antiterrorism unit in your own mind.

A wounded soldier home from war was at a supper honoring veterans when he was asked to share the most wonderful thing he'd experienced while on tour. After a moment's thought, he replied,

I was walking near my trench one day when I saw a young soldier lying on the ground, intently reading a book. I went up to him and asked what he was reading. He told me he was reading the Bible. Now, I had read the Bible for many years, and it never did me any good. But this soldier said to me, "Listen to what I am reading." And he read, "Let not your heart be troubled. In my Father's house are many mansions. I go to prepare a place for you. Neither let your heart be afraid."

The soldier explained that he responded to this Scripture by saying that he'd read it many times and it had never done him any good. "Give it up, man," he said. "Give it up." But the other soldier looked up from where he was reading on the ground and said, "If you knew what the Bible means to me, you would never ask me to give it up."

"As he spoke," said the soldier, "the light on his face was so bright. I never saw anything like it in my life. It just dazed me. I could not look at it for long, and so I turned and walked away."

Soon after that incident, a bomb fell near the place they had been speaking. When the dust cleared, he went to check on the young soldier who'd been reading the Bible. He found him fatally wounded, the Bible sticking out of his breast pocket.

"And here it is," the soldier told his audience as he held it up. "I want to say to you today who have gathered here at this occasion that the most wonderful thing I experienced during the war was the light on that young soldier's face. And more than that, I can say now that his Savior is my Savior too, for I read that book and I came to know the One who gave him peace in the midst of war."[10]

PEACE AND PRAYER

"Be anxious for nothing, but in everything by prayer and supplication, with thanksgiving, let your requests be made known to God" (Phil. 4:6). These are the most powerful words in the Bible concerning anxiety and prayer. In essence, Paul says the Christian life is composed of three circles. You can draw them in your imagination.

First is the Anxiety Circle, in which is "nothing." Second is the Prayer Circle, into which we must bring "everything." Finally, we have the Thanksgiving Circle, which must be filled with gratitude for everything God has done and is doing for us.

In other words, we must be anxious for nothing, prayerful for everything, and thankful for anything. This kind of praying never fails to produce!

Norman B. Harrison adds this: "The world worries, and has ample reason for doing so. It faces tremendous problems, with no real solution for them. But the Christian is very differently situated. He is 'not of this world.' Prayer maintains an otherworldly viewpoint, and he is spared the mental contagion."[11]

Some years ago I was at O'Hare International Airport after speaking at a conference in Chicago. I was flying out early in the morning, and I'd gotten to the airport with plenty of time only to discover my flight was delayed. A one-hour delay became a two-hour delay, so I went to the airline's club area to relax while I waited. When I checked in, I asked the woman at the desk if she knew what was going on with my flight.

"There's a storm hovering over Chicago," she said. "Would you like to see it?"

I went around the welcome desk, and on the computer screen

was an angry red mass swallowing up Chicago. No planes could land, and none could take off. So I settled in the club room, surrounded by windows, and watched the storm roll in. The rain and wind beat against the glass so hard I could actually see the windows shaking.

Suddenly I had a moment of clarity and truth. I was surrounded by a storm. In fact, I was sitting at the very center of the storm. But I was sitting in a comfortable chair with a cup of coffee in my hand, working on my computer and as safe as anyone could be. I was sheltered in the midst of the storm.

This is what God offers us when He gives us His peace. He offers us shelter from life's storms—all of them. He does not say He will make them go away or that they will never occur. He says simply that if we keep our minds and hearts on Him, He will give us perfect peace.

> *Hear my cry, O God;*
> *Attend to my prayer.*
> *From the end of the earth I will cry to You,*
> *When my heart is overwhelmed;*
> *Lead me to the rock that is higher than I.*
>
> *For You have been a shelter for me,*
> *A strong tower from the enemy.*
> *I will abide in Your tabernacle forever;*
> *I will trust in the shelter of Your wings.*
>
> —PSALM 61:1–4

CHAPTER 4

A LIFE OF ENDURANCE

Heavy weights, lifted fewer times in
succession, produce greater strength.
Lighter weights, lifted with more repetitions,
produce greater endurance.

Every morning when I'm home in San Diego, I go to a gym to work out with a trainer. His name is Todd Durkin, and he's one of the best trainers in the country—and one of the best things that's happened to me in recent years. Besides the fact that he's an incredible physical fitness expert and a dynamic motivator, Todd is also a Christ-follower.

Todd and I often talk about the similarities of physical training and spiritual training. Recently we were talking about weight lifting and the two different approaches athletes adopt when they're in training. Here's what I learned: Heavy weights, lifted fewer times in succession, produce greater strength. Lighter weights, lifted with more repetitions, produce greater endurance.

When it comes to life, most of us can lift a heavy weight if we only have to do it once or twice. In other words, major problems that come and then go away quickly may be painful, but they are usually manageable. For me, it's not the big problems that are the hardest.

For me, the problems that are the toughest to overcome are the problems that never seem to get solved . . . the ones that keep coming back. God wants us to be strong men and women of faith. To achieve that, I believe we must become men and women of resilience and endurance. If I cannot stand strong under the adversity of unrelenting pressure, I'll lose the joy of the journey.

The complexity of life can make our journey feel like the extreme obstacle courses and endurance runs we see on television. These games, whose competitors are people like us, are a metaphor for life today. The overwhelming pressures of our lives are symbolized by the near-impossible feats they must face. We identify with those "average superhuman" athletes. Their stories inspire and encourage us. If they can endure, we can endure. If they can hang on by their fingertips, maybe we can too.

There is a verse in the Bible that never ceases to challenge me. It's Hebrews 10:36, which states simply,

You have need of endurance.

Endurance is needed for godly living because few things about life are easy. While we shouldn't face each day with grim determination, we need something to carry us. Life requires a sustained determination to remain strong and faithful—step-by-step, day by day, and moment by moment. As Leo Tolstoy said in *War and Peace*,

"A man on a thousand-mile walk has to . . . say to himself every morning, 'Today I'm going to cover twenty-five miles and then rest up and sleep.'"[1]

A few days before I began writing this chapter, a young leader who works for me said, "The most important thing a leader does is define his reality."

What's your reality? Are you battling stubborn illness, physical weakness, or chronic pain? Is your athletic career plagued by recurring injuries? Maybe your heart is broken over a relationship that ended in disappointment. Perhaps you're worried about your marriage or anxious about your children. Are you grappling with tension in your workplace or division in your church? Are you exhausted? Working too hard? Perhaps you've made a mistake that troubles you, or you've been victimized in a way that's left you traumatized.

Peter told the people of his day, "Dear friends, don't be surprised at the fiery trials you are going through, as if something strange were happening to you" (1 Peter 4:12 NLT). I've told thousands of people the same thing. It's still some of the best advice out there.

Trials and sufferings aren't unique to you or me; they're the common lot of all humanity. That's why God wants us to cultivate the virtue of "longsuffering" in our lives (Gal. 5:22). That's why God wants to infuse us with a "can-do" attitude, with supernatural endurance, perseverance, and resilience. You and I cannot give up—not for a moment.

YOU HAVE NEED OF ENDURANCE

That exhortation in chapter 10 states the theme of the entire book of Hebrews. Every book in the Bible has its own special message to us, and I believe God placed Hebrews in the Bible near the end of the New Testament as an encouragement for us to persevere. If you're ever tempted to give up too soon—and it's always too soon to quit—study the book of Hebrews. Its main purpose is to give us reasons to keep going when we're weary of the road.

We don't know the name of the author of Hebrews, but we have a powerful clue about its background. In chapter 10, the writer identifies his audience. He's writing to people who had become Christ-followers years before and withstood an initial wave of opposition and brutal persecution. In the newfound flush of their faith, they endured and survived the onslaught. They were young and excited and, if necessary, ready to die for Christ.

But they did not have to die for Him in those earlier days of their faith, and in time the pressures subsided and things settled down. Persecution lessened and became manageable. They became comfortable, perhaps even complacent. Maybe they let down their guard a bit. They grew older.

Then one day their situation destabilized, and the threat of persecution rose again like a tidal wave swelling and heading right toward them. Things grew more dangerous by the moment. Once again these Christians faced the prospect of suffering greatly for their faith, but this time they were less infused with youthful zeal. They feared the future, and some of them were tempted to give up and revert to their old way of living.

The writer of the book of Hebrews alluded to this background story and exhorted his readers:

Remember those earlier days after you had received the light, when you endured in a great conflict full of suffering. Sometimes you were publicly exposed to insult and persecution; at other times you stood side by side with those who were so treated. You suffered along with those in prison and joyfully accepted the confiscation of your property, because you knew that you yourselves had better and lasting possessions. (Heb. 10:32–34 NIV)

Then come those verses I referred to earlier: God's challenge to you and me as we face our times of weariness and worry—Hebrews 10:35–36: "Therefore do not cast away your confidence, which has great reward. For you have need of endurance, so that after you have done the will of God, you may receive the promise."

You may not consider endurance one of your life skills—yet. But I promise you, endurance can be learned. Here from the fifty-eighth book of the Bible are seven key strategies to help you develop this virtue in your life.

EMBRACE YOUR ADVERSITY

The Bible is very clear about the way God teaches His children endurance: "Dear brothers and sisters, when troubles of any kind come your way, consider it an opportunity for great joy. For you know that when your faith is tested, your endurance has a chance to grow. So let it grow, for when your endurance is fully developed, you will be perfect and complete, needing nothing." (James 1:2–4 NLT).

The apostle Paul makes the same point in Romans 5: "We also glory in tribulations, knowing that tribulation produces perseverance; and perseverance, character; and character, hope" (vv. 3–4).

Adversity develops endurance. Endurance produces character. And people of character become people of hope. This is maturity in God's sight. People like this are complete, lacking nothing. This is the biblical secret of spiritual maturity.

When maturity reigns in your life, you have confidence, courage, and compassion. Confidence emanates from your heart, and it endures in you because you know who you are. Courage enables you to step into the unknown territory of selfless behavior because you're not only thinking about yourself. Your compassion becomes your hallmark, manifesting in a way that heals and changes those around you. Through trials and challenges, you persevere because your endurance has made you strong.

Isn't this what we want to teach our children? It's not easy for us as parents to watch our children try and fail, but we know how important it is for them to learn to persist in the right endeavors. Our job is to help them learn the rewards of perseverance.

Dr. Rachel Bryant, a clinical psychologist in New York, published an article entitled, "Children Learn When They Persevere," in which she stated the following:

> The power to persevere is one of the most important, and yet hardest, things to teach kids. If we teach them to persevere, then we give them their goals. If we don't teach them how to apply themselves, then all the love and tutoring in the world will never result in their reaching their potential. . . .
>
> Success requires ability, but ability is not enough. Many bright kids who sail through the early grades find themselves suddenly overwhelmed in fifth or sixth grade when the work requires much more effort. . . .
>
> Whatever the task, building a tower, gluing a model airplane, reading a social studies chapter or doing a page of math problems, first let your child know that you are pleased to see

them trying, and with your presence help them to stretch themselves just a few more minutes.[2]

At fifteen, American competitive swimmer Katie Ledecky stunned the swimming world by winning the gold medal in the 800-meter freestyle at the London Olympic Games. Four years later, she was the most decorated female athlete of the 2016 Olympic Games in Rio de Janeiro. As of this writing, she is a five-time Olympic gold medalist and has broken thirteen world records.

Ledecky's exceptional achievements cannot be overstated. The world has many champions, but Ledecky stands out because of her margin of victory. She competes in a league of her own.

"She's the greatest athlete in the world today by far," said Michael J. Joyner, a researcher for the Mayo Clinic in Rochester, Minnesota, specializing in human performance and physiology. "She's dominating by the widest margin in international sport, winning by 1 or 2 percent. . . . It's just absolutely remarkable."[3]

One percent or 2 percent may not sound like much, but Joyner explained that if Ledecky were running the 10,000 meters (the longest track and field event in the Olympics) and winning by 1 or 2 percent, she'd win by an unheard-of 100 meters. If she were a cyclist in the Tour de France, she'd win by an inconceivable 30 or 40 minutes, instead of a few minutes or even seconds.

How has Katie Ledecky become an enduring champion athlete? More important to our point here, how does she keep it up year after year?

Put simply: She trains for it, relentlessly. She is determined, disciplined, and willing to do the daily grind of practice and work to deliver exceptional performances again and again.

Ledecky's goal isn't to win and walk away, gold medal in hand.

Her goal is to always improve on her best and to continually break her own world records (which she's done repeatedly).[4] She receives expert coaching and she acts on it. She has a training plan designed to help her win, and she follows it. She embraces adversity as a training tool, choosing to train against—and frequently beat—competitive male swimmers. With enough accolades to retire and still be a legend, Ledecky continues to push herself to grow *so that she will endure.*

Like Katie Ledecky, we, too, can choose endurance. We can follow the coaching of the Son of Man and the apostles; we can follow a God-given training plan. And we too can embrace adversity as an opportunity to grow stronger.

We don't always know why life requires so much effort or why hardships arrive unexpectedly at our doorsteps; only eternity will reveal the purposes of some of our pain. But based on the message of Hebrews, plus James 1:2–4 and Romans 5:3–4, we know God wants to use our troubles to develop within us the quality of endurance, which represents the very core of character and maturity.

SURROUND YOURSELF WITH CHAMPIONS

Hebrews 12 begins with the word *therefore.* You've probably heard someone say, "Whenever you see the word *therefore*, you should try to discover what it's *there for.*" You usually discover the purpose of the "therefore" by looking backward into the previous verses. And that is the case in this instance.

Hebrews 11 is one of the most famous chapters in the entire Bible. It is sometimes called the "Hall of Fame" of the Bible or, better yet, the "Hall of Faith."

The people listed in this chapter are some of the greatest people of faith in history. One of the common characteristics of their lives was their persistence in the face of insurmountable obstacles. In chapter 12, we're challenged to allow these men and women to spur us on to greater levels of endurance, persistence, and accomplishment. Read these opening words: "Therefore we also, since we are surrounded by so great a cloud of witnesses . . . let us run with endurance the race that is set before us" (v. 1).

When the writer called these champions of faith "witnesses," we need to understand what he meant. There are two kinds of witnesses: "seeing" witnesses and "saying" witnesses. When people observe an accident, we say that they "witness" the event. They *see* it. But when they are summoned to court to talk about what they saw, they become "saying" witnesses. The witnesses of Hebrews 11 are "saying" witnesses.

In other words, they are not witnessing us as though they were leaning over the balcony of heaven and looking down at us. It means they are witnesses *to* us, inspiring us with the testimony of their faith, perseverance, and endurance.

Allow yourself to be spurred to strength and endurance by the examples of others, whether they are biblical characters, heroes in history, or people you personally know.

The name of the gym where I work out is Fitness Quest. When I walk in the door of that facility each morning, the first things I see are dozens of pictures of athletes. These are people who trained at this place and went on to success. As I begin my routine, I'm surrounded by some of the greatest athletes in the world! When I watch what they do to get ready for their seasons of competition, I am first embarrassed and then inspired. Just being around them makes me want to do better.

Maybe you're thinking, *I don't have any champions in my world.* Think again.

All the champions mentioned in Hebrews had been dead for centuries. Not one of the witnesses of Hebrews 11 was alive when that book was written.

But even though they were dead, they were still speaking through their written words and the records of their faith journeys. And so it is for us today. We are motivated, encouraged, and challenged by the lives of men and women who've been dead far longer than we've been alive.

Some people love to watch movies. Some love audiobooks. I love to read. I surround myself with champions by reading the stories of men and women who fought the same battles I am fighting and, through perseverance and endurance, won. It doesn't matter how you get your stories—film, TV, audiobooks, or printed books. Fill your world with champions by taking in the stories of people who inspire you.

Every man or woman with a gripping story has faced great adversity, sometimes far beyond the seeming boundaries of human endurance. One of the best—and most enjoyable—things we can do to develop endurance in our lives is to learn how it was achieved in the lives of others.

FIND YOUR PASSION AND PURSUE IT

This year I read the biography of Eliezer Ben Yehuda. I became interested in his story because of a street sign in Jerusalem that had his name on it. I asked a friend who he was and why he was important enough to have his name on a street sign in the center of one of the most important cities in the world. Instead of answering my question on the spot, my friend gave me a book about Ben Yehuda's life.

In the prologue of that book by Robert St. John is this statement:

[This] is the story of a [man] who . . . made enemies of his best friends, went to prison for his beliefs, was always on the verge of death from tuberculosis, yet fathered eleven children, gathered the material for a sixteen-volume dictionary unlike any other philological work ever conceived . . . and died while working on the word for "soul."[5]

Ben Yehuda devoted his life to the restoration of the Hebrew language to the Jewish people. For forty-one years he lived for nothing else! The story of his total dedication to accomplishing his vision is the definition of the word *endurance*. Because of him, the Jewish people no longer speak 150 separate languages. Their "national tongue is an unbroken circle; the national language of the state of Israel is Hebrew."[6]

When Ben Yehuda started to work on his dream, Hebrew was spoken only in religious contexts. It had not been used in daily life for two thousand years. But he lived to see the day when virtually every Jew in his country wrote on their census form, under "mother tongue," the word *Hebrew*.[7]

He lived to see the day when Hebrew was the language of the courts, the theater, of business, society, and public affairs.

During the forty-one years he had struggled to bring this about, he had often been called a "fanatic." After his death a eulogist added one word to that epithet, turning it into this epitaph:

Here Lies Eliezer Ben Yehuda
Faithful Fanatic[8]

When I finished reading that book, I felt a burning desire in my heart to be a "faithful fanatic"!

The biblical story of the apostle Paul rivals any modern biography. Like others we've mentioned, he lived for one purpose. In the first chapter of his letter to the Romans, he identified himself as "a slave of Christ Jesus" (v. 1 NLT).

In his second letter to the Corinthian believers, he detailed what he endured to carry out his assignment:

> I have . . . been whipped times without number, and faced death again and again. Five different times the Jewish leaders gave me thirty-nine lashes. Three times I was beaten with rods. Once I was stoned. Three times I was shipwrecked. Once I spent a whole night and a day adrift at sea. I have traveled on many long journeys. I have faced danger from rivers and from robbers. I have faced danger from my own people, the Jews, as well as from the Gentiles. I have faced danger in the cities, in the deserts, and on the seas. And I have faced danger from men who claim to be believers but are not. I have worked hard and long, enduring many sleepless nights. I have been hungry and thirsty and have often gone without food. I have shivered in the cold, without enough clothing to keep me warm. (2 Cor. 11:23–27 NLT)

Paul knew what he was talking about when he wrote these words to his young protégé, Timothy: "You therefore must endure hardship as a good soldier of Jesus Christ" (2 Tim. 2:3).

GET RID OF WHAT'S HOLDING YOU BACK

Like a swimmer or runner preparing to compete, let's strip off anything that weighs us down or slows our forward progress. "Let us lay aside every weight, and the sin which so easily ensnares us" (Heb. 12:1).

This is a great time to pause for a little self-examination. Is unbelief hindering you? Is some habit stalling your spiritual momentum? Is some sin demoralizing you? Are you sulking when you should be singing? What change do you need to make if you're going to keep going in the strength of the Lord?

Within the context of Hebrews 10–12, the greatest hindrance to the Christians was creeping unbelief. These believers had forgotten the power and the promises of Jesus Christ, and they were thinking of reverting back to their old life to avoid the coming wave of persecution. But the writer of Hebrews warned them against that, saying that Jesus was better than anything they had known in the past and that He would never leave them nor forsake them.

God gave us the book of Hebrews so we could examine ourselves when we grow discouraged, recognize and confess our unbelief, strip it away, and get rid of the sin of doubt that so easily entangles us.

We all know from painful experience that unbelief erodes our confidence in God's ability to overrule our situations, and it sows the seeds of self-pity in our hearts. Instead of saying, "The Lord can handle this!" we say, "Oh, why is this happening to me? What am I going to do?"

Self-pity is a particularly damaging form of unbelief. We become self-centered instead of Savior-centered. We no longer feel God is in control of our lives, so we let our focus shift from His sovereignty to our struggles. People who feel sorry for themselves enter a negative cycle that's difficult to break.

If you're feeling discouraged enough to give up, ask yourself if self-pity has begun growing in your heart like mold in a damp basement. Confess it. Throw off every weight and the sin that so easily entangles, and realize that with Jesus' help, you can meet the challenges and go on. Don't focus on what you have lost but on what you have left, because what you have left includes all the power and promises of God through Jesus Christ.

Sometimes what holds us back is a "who" and not a "what." Sometimes there are people in our lives who prevent us from growing into men and women of endurance. If we're honest with ourselves, we usually know who they are. But often we'll go to any lengths to avoid acknowledging it—even to ourselves.

Why? Because relationships are fraught with emotion and with our own expectations. We linger in unhealthy relationships for many reasons: force of habit, convenience, avoidance of change, fear of being alone, even a conviction that we are "fixing" them. Or maybe we stay for reasons we believe are good; we tell ourselves we're being loyal, or we explain away the behavior because we understand why this person is the way her or she is, or perhaps we believe to let go of the relationship would be un-Christian.

If this sounds familiar, ask yourself these tough questions: *Am I truly helping my friend to move forward, or is my friend holding me back? Is my friend causing me to stay stuck at the level I am, or even causing me to move backward?*

If your friend is holding you back, then you are paying a price you cannot afford. It is profoundly difficult to move forward when someone is sucking the energy and positivity out of you. You must move on from those who are not champions or who are not striving to become champions. Is that Christian to do? It absolutely is.

All of us struggle with this at some point in our lives. The circle of friends that truly sustains each of us is small, and there's not room in that circle for everybody. As you grow in faith and God gives you more influence, this can become even more of an issue.

Surround yourself with people who will lift you up or who want to work with you as you lift them up. Open your heart and your conversations to talk about God, about faith and Scripture. When you begin to do this, God will give you the discernment to know which relationships to pursue and which to move on from.

DON'T EVEN THINK ABOUT QUITTING

Endurance requires a strong sense of resolve. We have to make up our minds that we will not falter or give up. Hebrews 12:1 puts it this way: "Let us run with endurance the race that is set before us."

The phrase "let us" occurs thirteen times in Hebrews, and it speaks to our choices. Yes, God helps us, and we can never do it without His grace. But we have a part too.

Harriet Beecher Stowe, a deeply spiritual woman and the author of *Uncle Tom's Cabin*, said: "When you get into a tight place, and everything goes against you till it seems as though you couldn't hang on a minute longer, *never give up then*, for that's just the place and time that the tide'll turn."[9]

Grit is a book written by an amazing writer named Angela Duckworth. "Drawing on her own powerful story as the daughter of a scientist who frequently noted her lack of 'genius,' Duckworth, now a celebrated researcher and professor, describes her early eye-opening stints in teaching, business consulting, and neuro-science, which led to the hypothesis that what really drives success is not 'genius' but a unique combination of passion and long-term perseverance."[10]

She defined what it means to have grit as, simply, "to be gritty."

"To be gritty is to keep putting one foot in front of the other. To be gritty is to hold fast to an interesting and purposeful goal. To be gritty is to invest, day after week after year, in challenging practice. To be gritty is to fall down seven times, and rise eight."[11]

Angela shared dozens of stories about people who paid the price to be successful through determination and perseverance. One of my favorites is about actor Will Smith, who explains his success in the entertainment industry this way:

> The only thing that I see that is distinctly different about me is: I'm not afraid to die on a treadmill. I will not be outworked, period. You might have more talent than me, you might be smarter than me. . . . You might be all of those things. You got it on me in nine categories. But if we get on the treadmill together, there's two things. You're getting off first, or I'm going to die. It's really that simple.[12]

The late novelist Irving Stone studied some of the greatest and most interesting characters in history and wrote biographical novels about them—people like Vincent van Gogh, Michelangelo, and Abraham Lincoln. After years of research, he said this: "I write about people who sometime in their life have a vision or dream of something that should be accomplished, and then they go to work. They are beaten over the head, knocked down, vilified, and for years they get nowhere. But every time they're knocked down they stand up. You cannot destroy these people. And at the end of their lives they've accomplished some modest part of what they set out to do."[13]

The Bible says we must run with perseverance the race that is set before us. We mustn't give up. We can't all be Olympic athletes; but we can all be soldiers of the cross, and we can all run the race set before us with perseverance, looking unto Jesus, who is the author and finisher of our faith. Obstacle courses are no obstacle for Him who can do all things, or for those who can do all things through Christ who strengthens them.

NEVER STOP ACHIEVING

Many people have gone through periods of discouragement and weariness in their bodies and souls. We all have. I know people who spent their whole lives preparing for a time of retirement, expecting to enjoy their sunset years, travel with their spouses, and see the world. And none of it happened. In some cases disability and death intruded; in others there were financial reversals. Like the Hebrews of New Testament days, they were tempted to lose heart.

Don't quit now! Trust God, press on, and win the victory in Christ. God's enduring grace will enable you to reach forward to those things that are ahead with faith and victory. And you don't have to do it alone. You've got the inspiration coming from God's heroes of the faith, the examination that leads us to throw off hindering weights and sins, the God-commanded determination to run our race with patience, and the God-given anticipation of looking unto Jesus and the joy He sets before us. "Do not cast away your confidence, which has great reward. For you have need of endurance, so that after you have done the will of God, you may receive the promise" (Heb. 10:35–36).

On our national television program in early 2017, I told the story of Erik Weihenmayer, the first blind man to successfully climb to the top of Mount Everest, the highest point on earth. The story of that herculean accomplishment was told in the book *Touch the Top of the World*.[14] Shortly after that television program aired, I received a letter from Erik's father. Here's what he wrote:

> As he was completing his Everest descent, his team leader spoke these words to him which profoundly affected the next chapter in his life: *Don't let Everest be the greatest thing you ever do*, meaning do not create a mausoleum of your trophies and retire on your laurels. Many years later, after 6 years of intense training, he solo kayaked the mighty rapids of the Grand Canyon, 277 miles, a feat more difficult than Everest.
>
> But Erik's greatest accomplishment, in his mind, is the founding of No Barriers, devoted to helping challenged people reach for that next rung on the ladder to become their best selves, to add their energy and passion and dreams to this world which needs them so badly. After 12 years of operation, No Barriers impacts 5,000 people annually—injured soldiers, paraplegics, amputees, stroke victims, those with mental challenges, blind, etc. Imagine a person without arms kayaking, a person without limbs climbing Kilimanjaro, paraplegics mountain biking, a one-arm violinist playing Amazing Grace on a mountain peak. This is No Barriers.

I am scheduled to meet Erik in the near future, and I can't wait to be in the presence of this champion who, in spite of his blindness, climbed the highest mountain in the world and continues to do the seemingly impossible.

STAY FOCUSED ON THE GOAL

Endurance takes anticipation. We must focus on Jesus and the life He offers us. Hebrews 12:1–3 ends with a glorious upward shift:

> Let us run with endurance the race God has set before us. We do this by keeping our eyes on Jesus, the champion who initiates and perfects our faith. Because of the joy awaiting him, he endured the cross, disregarding its shame. Now he is seated in the place of honor beside God's throne. Think of all the hostility he endured from sinful people; then you won't become weary and give up. (NLT)

Toward the end of his life, the great apostle Paul spoke of his goal. Here's what he said: "I press toward the goal for the prize of the upward call of God in Christ Jesus" (Phil. 3:14).

Bible teacher John Phillips wrote: "We must consider Him, and that will keep us from drooping, keep us from discouragement. He is the great stimulant to nerve the soul to the utmost. When tempted to give in, we need only think, 'He's watching!' What a difference it makes, even in human affairs, to know that in some great contest a loved one is eagerly watching to see us win!"[15]

Jesus endured the cross because He anticipated the joy that would follow, and we must fix our gaze on Him. We endure because He endured, and He endures still, both now and forever. In fact, it is no overstatement to say that our ability to endure whatever life throws at us is rooted and grounded in the enduring quality of God, which is spoken of throughout the Bible, and especially in the Psalms.

Life requires endurance, but we don't have to persevere in our own strength or keep going on the sheer basis of willpower alone. We fix our eyes on Jesus, and we endure and thrive because of His endurance. We are "strengthened with all might, according to His glorious power, for all patience and longsuffering with joy" (Col. 1:11).

In his famous business book, *Good to Great*, Jim Collins told this story:

> The coaching staff of a high school cross-country running team . . . got together for dinner after winning its second state championship in two years. The program had been transformed in the previous five years from good (top twenty in the state) to great (consistent contenders for the state championship, on both the boys' and girls' teams).
>
> "I don't get it," said one of the coaches. "Why are we so successful? We don't work any harder than other teams. And what we do is just so simple. Why does it work?"
>
> He was referring to the Hedgehog Concept of the program, captured in the simple statement: We run best at the end. We run best at the end of workouts. We run best at the end of races. And we run best at the end of the season, when it counts the most. Everything is geared to this simple idea, and the coaching staff knows how to create this effect better than any other team in the state. For example, they place a coach at the 2-mile mark (of a 3.1-mile race) to collect data as the runners go past. . . . Then the coaches calculate not how fast the runners go, but *how many competitors they pass at the end of the race*, from mile 2 to the finish. . . . The kids learn how to pace themselves, and race with confidence: "We run best at the end," they think at the end of a hard race. "So, if I'm hurting bad, then my competitors must hurt a whole lot worse!"[16]

I believe we are near the end, and therefore we need to run as never before . . . we need to run with perseverance and endurance. We need to run to win!

> *And do this, knowing the time, that now it is high*
> *time to awake out of sleep; for now our salvation*
> *is nearer than when we first believed.*

> —ROMANS 13:11

CHAPTER 5

A LIFE OF COMPASSION

Sympathy is something you feel;
compassion is something you show
or, better yet, something you do.

When Sylvie de Toledo's sister died from a drug overdose, she left behind her eight-year-old son, Kevin. Sylvie's parents immediately took Kevin in and raised him from then on. It wasn't easy, and Sylvie, a social worker, saw the toll it took on her parents' marriage and health.

In her work, Sylvie was seeing more and more grandparents dealing with the same situation. She knew they felt isolated and alone. Moved to help, she started a small support group for about ten grandparents raising their grandchildren. Soon so many grandparents were attending that Sylvie had to do more. So she started her own nonprofit, Grandparents as Parents.

Almost thirty years later Grandparents as Parents helps more than three thousand families a year, providing guidance, financial assistance, legal advice, and emotional support.

Today nearly three million children in America are being raised by their grandparents. Many of those grandparents live on fixed incomes and are unprepared for the financial and emotional costs of raising their children's children.

"We've seen countless families who maxed out credit cards and used all their savings before they even ask for help," Sylvie said.

Her organization has become "a one-stop shop for relative caregivers." More than 90 percent of those they help are grandparents; but aunts, uncles, siblings, and close friends have stepped up to care for children when their biological parents can't, and Sylvie helps them all.

"So many times, these families are completely overwhelmed. The kids come to them with a dirty diaper and a T-shirt that's way too big for them."

Grandparents as Parents saves families, keeps thousands of children out of foster care, and works to prevent siblings from being separated. But Sylvie credits caregivers for being the true heroes.

"It's really the grandparents and relatives doing this that deserve the recognition for putting their own lives on hold," she said. "I was able to plant a seed with something that happened in my own family. . . . From a family tragedy, something wonderful has happened."[1]

Compassion is about the moment. It's about what I have in hand—money, talent, encouragement, or a shoulder to cry on—that will meet another person's need. Compassion is about those times in our lives when God intends for us to be the healer, the helper, the hero in the life of another person.

Sylvie de Toledo acted with compassion for grandparents going through what she'd seen her own parents struggle with. Beyond helping them through her job as a social worker, she wanted them to know they weren't alone and to have a community where they could share ideas and support each other. Sylvie did what she could with what she had. And what she began, God multiplied.

In all of human literature, no greater illustration of what it means to be compassionate exists than the story Jesus told about the Good Samaritan. That story, recorded only in Luke's gospel, teaches us that we can never separate our relationship with God from our relationship with our fellow man.

In the previous chapters of this book, I have told the biblical story about the discipline we are studying, and then I have concluded the chapter with some practical how-to suggestions for putting that discipline into practice. But in this chapter, the story and the strategies are so intertwined that we will not be able to separate them. So in the pages that follow, we'll discover how to live a life of compassion *as* we walk through the story of the Good Samaritan. After all, it's often the stories we encounter that change our hearts and motivate us to action.

I want to begin by eliminating the things that can often be mistaken for compassion.

COMPASSION IS NOT ACADEMIC

Luke introduces the story of the Good Samaritan with the Lord being asked a question by a "certain lawyer" who, testing Jesus (and showing off as well), stood up and asked what he had to do to inherit eternal life.

Jesus answered by asking the question of him, "What is written in the law? What is your reading of it?"

And the lawyer answered, saying, "'You shall love the LORD your God with all your heart, with all your soul, with all your strength, and with all your mind,' and 'your neighbor as yourself.'"

"And He said to him, 'You have answered rightly; do this and you will live.'

"But he, wanting to justify himself, said to Jesus, 'And who is my neighbor?'" (Luke 10:25–29).

This "certain lawyer" had studied the Law of Moses. He was what we might call today a theologian. The religious lawyers of Jesus' day loved to discuss the urgent social problems of their time . . . but they didn't want to do anything about them. They often framed their discussions to avoid feeling personal responsibility.

This lawyer had sufficient knowledge of the Scripture to recite one of the most important theses of the Old Testament from memory. But he didn't know what it really meant, nor did he know how to apply it to his life. You see, it's not possible to love your neighbor and not know who he is. So when he asked Jesus, "Who is my neighbor?" he gave himself away.

In his little book on compassion, Charles Swindoll told a story that reminds us of our potential to replicate this New Testament incident even today. This event occurred on the campus of an evangelical seminary, the very grounds where future ministers were in training. A Greek class was given an assignment to study Luke 10:25–37, the same Good Samaritan story we are considering:

> These young theologs were to do an in-depth analysis of the biblical text, observing and commenting on all the major terms and syntactical factors worth mentioning. Each student was

to write his own translation after having done the work on his commentary.

As is true in most language classes, a couple or three of the students cared more about the practical implications of the assignment than its intellectual stimulation. The morning the work was to be turned in, these three teamed up and carried out a plan to prove their point. One volunteered to play the part of an alleged victim. They tore his shirt and trousers, rubbed mud, catsup, and other realistic-looking ingredients across his "wounds," marked up his eyes and face so he hardly resembled himself, then placed him along the path that led from the dormitory to the Greek classroom. While the other two hid and watched, he groaned and writhed, simulating great pain.

Not one student stopped. They walked around him, stepped over him, and said different things to him.

But nobody stooped over to help. What do you want to bet their academic work was flawless . . . and insightful . . . and handed in on time?[2]

We too can be tempted to be "students of compassion." We can enjoy stories written about it and movies made about it. We can applaud those who practice it. But we haven't shown compassion to anyone unless we act on it.

COMPASSION IS NOT ABSTRACT

Jesus begins His story in verse 30: "A certain man went down from Jerusalem to Jericho, and fell among thieves, who stripped him of his clothing, wounded him, and departed, leaving him half dead."

Jerusalem is some 2,300 feet above sea level, and Jericho is about 800 feet below sea level. So the road where the traveler was left for dead was steep, filled with narrow gorges and short curves that provided excellent hiding places for robbers.

The lawyer would have known how dangerous this road was. He'd have been able to picture in his mind the bruised and wounded body of the traveler. In telling him this story, Jesus refused to allow the lawyer to deal with compassion in the abstract.

And Jesus will not allow us to be abstract about the identity of our neighbor today either.

In 2003, California experienced its largest wildfire in more than a century. The Southern California Cedar Fire was a confluence of fifteen individual fires intensified by the hot, dry Santa Ana winds. It destroyed more than 2,300 homes and incinerated more than 280,000 acres. Many families in our congregation lost their homes to that fire.

In the mountains just above our church campus is a small community called Crest. Almost every family in Crest was severely impacted by the cedar fire. These people were our neighbors, and they desperately needed our help.

For the next six weeks, we adopted the Crest community. We collected blankets, clothing, shoes, and toys. One of our couples, David and Debbie St. John, made Crest their home for those six weeks. Debbie spent long hours every day helping people fight their way back from this awful fire.[3]

One of my most vivid memories of that time was being a part of one of our ministry teams for a day. An important act of compassion we offered families who lost their homes was helping them clean off the concrete slab their home had stood on so the debris could be trucked away and rebuilding could begin.

As a team we helped these people sift through the burnt debris of what had once been their home, looking for items of value that might have withstood the fire. I'm talking about jewelry, occasionally even some pictures. When we finished, we invited the family who'd lived in that home to join hands with our team in a circle of prayer. I never had such a hard time getting through a prayer as I did that day. And I never felt so useful to God as a pastor and as an individual.

We have people in our church today who first felt the love of God during that fire. Before the fire, they were our neighbors. Because of the fire, we became neighbors to them.

COMPASSION IS NOT AFRAID

Jesus continued the story, saying that by chance a certain priest came down the road (v. 31). Again, Jesus' listeners would have known the backstory. The temple required twenty-four teams of priests, with each team allowed to serve in the temple proper for only two weeks a year. The priest who traveled down that road would have been one of the twelve thousand priests living in Jericho at that time, and he might have just finished his two-week stint in the temple. As he walked along, he was remembering and reliving the excitement and joy of his fourteen days in the holiest place on earth. His desire to serve God out of purity and holiness was at an all-time high.

Suddenly this priest sees the wounded man, and he's forced to confront the neediness and dirtiness of the real world. And he's afraid!

There was no way the priest could be sure if the man was alive or dead, and he couldn't afford to find out. By the religious law of that time, if the man was dead and the priest touched him, the priest would have been ceremonially unclean for seven days. So the priest made a decision; he put the afterglow of his temple experience above the claims of suffering humanity. Not only did he pass by the wounded man; he passed by on the other side of the road.

COMPASSION IS NOT ANALYTICAL

It's easy to become paralyzed when we analyze. Because we are busy analyzing *everything* that needs to be done, we fail to do *anything*. This paralysis by analysis is what happened to the next character in Jesus' story.

Jesus continued: "Likewise a Levite, when he arrived at the place, came and looked, and passed by on the other side" (v. 32).

The Levite was a servant of the temple, a minister of religious worship and an interpreter of the law. He should have been eager to help this distressed soul. He had the opportunity, he had the knowledge, and he even had a bit more curiosity.

The Levite actually took the trouble to go near and look at the victim. But then he did the unthinkable. He crossed to the other side of the road and made no attempt to help. He probably knew the man was alive and suffering yet, heartlessly, did nothing.

Some have thought the priest who passed by on the other side thought to himself, *I'll leave this to the Levite who's following close after me.* And the Levite thought since the priest passed him by, stopping must not be a good thing for him to do either, so he also passed by. The priest did not serve because of the Levite, and the Levite did not serve because of the priest. And all the while the poor man who was beaten and bruised was lying there dying.

The priest and the Levite illustrate the fact that religious work does not make the worker religious. They probably were both very good at their official work in the service of God, but because they lacked compassion, they did not—could not—understand what serving God really meant.

Now that we've discovered what compassion *isn't*, what is it?

COMPASSION CAN SURPRISE YOU

Now Jesus said:

> "But a certain Samaritan, as he journeyed, came where he was. And when he saw him, he had compassion. So he went to him and bandaged his wounds, pouring on oil and wine; and he set him on his own animal, brought him to an inn, and took care of him. On the next day, when he departed, he took out two denarii, gave them to the innkeeper, and said to him, 'Take care of him; and whatever more you spend, when I come again, I will repay you.'" (Luke 10:33–35)

To fully understand this story, you have to know that there were few people Jesus could have used as an example of compassion who would have shocked His listeners more—especially the "certain lawyer." The Samaritan was a foreigner, with strange clothes and an odd accent. The Samaritans hated the Jews, and the Jews hated the Samaritans. He wasn't like the others in the story, with whom the listeners could identify.

Out of all those who could have been neighbors to this man, the one who became a neighbor out of compassion was a despised foreigner, a Samaritan. This thought would have been particularly intolerable to the lawyer. Picture the moment when Jesus asked the lawyer at the end of the story which of the three men had demonstrated that he was a neighbor, and the lawyer said, "He who showed mercy on him" (v. 37). He could not even mention the fact that he was a Samaritan.

Like the Savior, the Samaritan brought himself near and made himself a neighbor. And by what he did that day, he made his nationality forever synonymous with kindness and good works. When you drive through the cities of our land and pass the Good Samaritan Hospital, the Good Samaritan Clinic, the Good Samaritan Retirement Center, the Good Samaritan Church, you realize the reach of this New Testament story. Not only into our hearts but across millennia into our physical world, his compassion continues to be honored.

COMPASSION IS ABOUT WHAT YOU SEE

The priest, the Levite, and the Samaritan all *looked* at the traveler. But only the Good Samaritan *saw* him.

For Jesus, who is the ultimate Good Samaritan, compassion began with what He saw. On many occasions in the Gospels, Jesus' compassion was linked to seeing. In Matthew 9, He *saw* a crowd of people who were weary and confused, and He had compassion on them. In Matthew 14, Jesus *saw* another great multitude, and He healed their sick. In Mark 6, Jesus *saw* those who were like sheep without a shepherd, and He was moved with compassion to teach them.

When Jesus looked at those around, He saw opportunities to help. And in seeing, He was moved to compassion in many ways.

He was compassionate toward those who were lost spiritually; He was compassionate toward the sick; He was compassionate toward the needy; He was compassionate toward widows and mothers.

He touched lepers, cured sick people, befriended social pariahs, and cherished children. His last acts were to pray for the forgiveness of His murderers and then to look beside Him and feel compassion for a dying thief whom He encouraged and assured of salvation. In His deepest hours of agony, never for a moment did He take a break from showing compassion to others. The more difficult His life became, the more people crowded around Him with demands, and the closer He moved to a torturous death, the more loving, compassionate, and forgiving He became.[4]

When Jesus saw broken humanity, His heart was moved with compassion. And in this story the Samaritan saw this broken traveler through the eyes of Jesus and had compassion for him.

And seeing him, he had to do something.

COMPASSION IS ABOUT WHAT YOU DO

The Good Samaritan did more than observe the fallen traveler as the others had done. If I have counted correctly, he performed nine different acts of compassion on this wounded stranger. Not only that, he did this at his peril. By getting involved in this situation and tarrying on the road, the Samaritan risked the same kind of treatment that had befallen the wounded man.

Genuine love always involves action. Unlike the priest, the Samaritan touched the traveler with hands of kindness and compassion. No ceremonial reason restrained him. He bandaged the stranger's wounds, bathed his sores, and helped him to a safe place where he could recover. This was true compassion on display. This was compassion at work.

"But whoever has this world's goods, and sees his brother in need, and shuts up his heart from him, how does the love of God abide in him? My little children, let us not love in word or in tongue, but in deed and in truth" (1 John 3:17–18). Consider this story:

> A Christian leader was invited to speak to a large gathering of women in an affluent church. Before he spoke, the woman leading the meeting relayed an urgent financial need from one of the church's missionaries. She asked if the speaker would lead the group in prayer for God to supply the need.
>
> He came to the podium and shocked the group by saying he would not lead the group in the requested prayer, but he would do something else. He would contribute all the money he had in his pockets to meet the need if all the women in the group would do the same. If, when that money was collected and counted, funds were still lacking, he would be happy to lead in prayer for God to supply the rest.[5]

You can guess what happened. When the money was collected, there was more than enough to meet the missionary's emergency need.

Prayer can be compassionate, but compassion requires more than prayer. When it comes to compassion, sometimes God intends for us to answer our own prayers—in the moment.

As I was writing this chapter, a reporter asked me to explain the difference between sympathy and compassion. I told him sympathy is something you feel; compassion is something you show or, better yet, something you do!

In the Bible, God exhibits great kindness toward those who are in trouble or who are physically or emotionally afflicted. A vast number of verses speak about the kindness of God toward those in poverty. The kindness of God is often exhibited in a special way toward the poor; and God's kindness is specifically directed to those who hope in Him, who revere and fear Him, and who wait for Him.

Isn't it interesting that the people at whom we frequently direct respect and kindness in our culture are often different from the special people to whom God shows kindness? God emphasizes the importance of those whom we would consider to be "down-and-out." When God exhibits His kindness, He never seeks anything in return. It's a pure act of love on His part.

COMPASSION IS ABOUT HOW YOU DO IT

When Jesus asked the lawyer at the end of the story which of the three men had demonstrated that he was a neighbor, the lawyer said, "The one who showed mercy."

That's what the Samaritan did! He showed mercy on this needy traveler. He cleansed his wounds with wine. (At that time, the alcohol content of the wine was often used to cauterize wounds and cleanse them.)

Then the Samaritan poured oil on his wounds and bound up his wounds in bandages so that they could begin to heal. He delivered his compassion to this man with great mercy and care.

In one of the key New Testament verses on the subject of compassion, we're instructed about the manner in which compassion is to be given: "Having compassion for one another; love as brothers, be tenderhearted, be courteous" (1 Peter 3:8).

Compassion contains empathy; "love as brothers." When we empathize, we feel what it would be like to stand in another person's shoes. I've been blessed to be able to teach in some of the places in Israel where Jesus showed His compassion. Being in these places deepened my belief that compassion has to do with suffering of the soul, even with anguish and agony of the soul.

Through your own challenges and suffering, you develop an understanding of how someone else feels, of what a situation might be like. Through this understanding you can enter into another person's pain and suffering. And because of that, you have to do something for him. You feel what he feels, and you try to find a way to make it not so bad.

Tenderness is also an essential quality of compassion; we're instructed to "be tenderhearted." Tenderness is a personal feeling of gentle care, as when a parent feels tenderly toward his or her child. It's an aspect of compassion that communicates genuine concern and kindness between individuals. It may be a child you send to school whom you've never met; it may be a grieving parent you know; it may be your own neighbor; but in that moment, it is compassion that moves you to act, as one loving being to another. At its core, compassion is personal.

And, finally, we're told to "be courteous." Compassion is always courteous and respectful—in the action you take for others and through what is in your heart when you do it. Courtesy is the language of respect. How you speak to and interact with someone for whom you feel compassion reveals whether or not you see this person as deserving of dignity and respect. If you recognize this person as a child of God, respect follows.

Sometimes compassion leads to forgiveness. Some of the greatest acts of compassion occur when you have a choice to make; will you react with compassion and kindness and build a bridge of love, or not?

The world needs compassion and kindness. But we can narrow the scope even further. Your world needs kindness. Your home needs kindness. Where people are living in close proximity, kindness sometimes gets lost.

In the New Testament the instruction given to the church is also often given to the home. When Ephesians 4:32 says, "Be kind to one another, tenderhearted, forgiving one another, even as God in Christ forgave you," that's also directed at the home.

We need to be tenderhearted, kind, and forgiving. The fruit of the Spirit is tested in that laboratory we call the family. If you can have compassion and make it work there, it will work anywhere on the face of the earth.

When I started at the church where I pastor now, I was going through some very difficult times. There was a lot of turmoil in the church. Being new, I didn't know other men in the ministry. One day I got a call from the pastor of another local church who said, "Hey, I know a little about what you're going through. I don't need any of the details. I just want to say hang in there. And I want you to know that I'm here if you need a friend."

Even more amazing, a few days later he was getting ready to go on vacation, and he called again. He explained that he was heading out of town and gave me his number. "I just wanted you to have my number in case you need me."

It's hard to express what this meant to me at that time. That simple act of genuine compassion lifted me up, renewed my strength, and let me know I wasn't alone. I've never forgotten it.

COMPASSION IS ABOUT WHAT IT COSTS YOU

Sometimes compassion costs us time; sometimes it costs us more. But true compassion doesn't weigh the cost first; it simply responds to human suffering with loving kindness:

The Samaritan gave his eyes to the traveler when he looked upon him with concern. He gave his heart to the traveler when he felt true compassion for him. He gave his beast and his own feet to the traveler when he let him ride, willingly walking beside his own animal. He gave his hands to the traveler when he bound up his wounds. He gave his time to the traveler when he postponed his own schedule to stay with him on that first critical night. Finally, he gave his money to the traveler when he paid for his stay at the inn.[6]

Jesus is teaching us that when we love somebody, we give of ourselves to him or her. We share time, money, possessions, and priorities.

At the beginning of the story, the lawyer asked Jesus, "Who is my neighbor?" (Luke 10:29).

At the end of the story, Jesus asked the lawyer who was neighbor to the wounded man.

The conversation turned from "Who is my neighbor?" to "Who is neighbor to him?" In other words, the key question at the end of the story, and the key element of compassion, is not "Who is going to help me?" but "Who am I going to help?"

And then the Master said, "Go and do likewise" (v. 37).

And there it is. There is our command: to be compassionate, to give of ourselves, and to emulate the stranger in the foreign land who cared more than the temple priests and administrators, who cared more than the theologian who discoursed but did not act.

In saying, "Go and do likewise," Jesus was giving the lawyer a choice and a chance. The choice was to go and do as the Good Samaritan did. The chance was to become a person of compassion. For compassion is easily learned—if we choose to learn it.

Andrew Arroyo is the founder and president of a large California real estate company. He and his family attend the church that I pastor, and over the last several months we have become good friends. One Friday afternoon he was making a hurried stop at a storage unit to pick up supplies for his annual company award event. While he was loading his car with decorations, including stanchions, red velvet ropes, and a red carpet for his associates to walk on as they entered the event, he noticed an elderly woman outside the door of the storage facility.

Very methodically, the woman was laying down blankets on the concrete next to a shopping cart. It was obvious she was preparing to spend the night there. As he worked and watched, he felt he was watching his own mother or grandmother preparing to sleep outdoors on a cold winter's night.

Andrew approached the woman and handed her one of the Subway gift cards he always carries with him. And that could have been the end of it. After all, the work of recognizing and appreciating his employees was important and caring work as well.

Instead, Andrew opened the door to a conversation and learned her story. She was a seventy-three-year-old retired banker. Widowed, she received Social Security and a pension, but the total wasn't enough to make ends meet. For fifteen years she'd lived in her van. A year earlier it was towed, and she didn't have enough to reclaim it. She'd been on the streets ever since.

For a moment Andrew was conflicted, but then his compassion moved him to action. He told the woman he wanted to help her, and the first thing he would do was get her a hotel room until he could figure out a permanent solution. He turned to go back to loading his supplies, and an idea struck him. "Could I roll out this red carpet for you?" he asked.

The woman was speechless. He quickly set up the ropes and rolled the carpet out. And this one spontaneous act brought her to life. Her eyes filled with tears as she shared memories of going to the opera, of dancing, of being a talented seamstress in her younger days and designing her own evening dresses. It was a conversation Andrew will never forget.

That night Andrew found the woman a hotel room. For the next six weeks he paid the bill while he looked for a travel trailer she could move into. He found one, bought it, and a member of his company let him park it on his land. Eventually he found an RV park where the trailer could be permanently moved.

As I write this chapter, this woman still lives in the RV park, her pension and Social Security enough to meet her needs.

Why did he do all this for a stranger? In a letter he wrote to me, Andrew explained:

> I'm tired of helping people with a temporary solution and then saying, "I will pray for you." Loving someone who loves you is easy. Loving a complete stranger or someone who uses and takes advantage of you is not (Luke 6:37). I've discovered this form of unconditional love (*agape*) is where the true blessing of mercy and compassion resides. It takes a supernatural kind of love to conquer the flesh that says, "This person doesn't deserve my love," or "This person annoys me or has offended me; therefore, I don't want them in my life." Yet Christ never ceases loving us despite our own multitude of sins.[7]

Andrew Arroyo encountered a desperately poor woman. She had abundant needs, and he had abundant ability to meet those needs. Moved by compassion to do something more permanent than just give her a meal, he made a remarkable commitment. Without knowing the clear path forward, he acted. What started with getting a woman off the street for a night is an ongoing, compassionate commitment he is able and happy to shoulder.

The world has a right to expect followers of Jesus to be like their Master. You may not be able to heal the sick or feed the hungry multitudes the way Jesus did. But that's okay—He doesn't expect that of you. He only expects you to be a genuine channel of His compassion to those who need Him today.

A STORY TO REMEMBER

Bill was a wild-haired, T-shirt-wearing, barefoot college student. He was esoteric and brilliant, and while attending college, he became a Christian.

Across the street from the campus was a well-dressed, very conservative church that wanted to develop a ministry to the students at the college, but they were not sure how to go about it.

One day Bill decided to go into that church. He walked in with no shoes, jeans, a T-shirt, and wild hair. The service had already started, so Bill started down the aisle, looking for a seat. But the church was packed, and he couldn't find one. By now people were looking a bit uncomfortable, but no one said anything.

Bill got closer and closer to the pulpit, and when he realized there were no seats, he just sat down right in the aisle on the carpet.

By now the congregation was really uncomfortable, and the tension in the air was thick. About this time, from way at the back of the large church, a deacon was slowly making his way toward Bill. The deacon was in his eighties, with silver-gray hair and a pocket watch, a godly man who was very elegant, dignified, and walked with a cane.

It took a long time for the man to reach the boy. The church fell utterly silent, except for the clicking of the man's cane. All eyes were focused on him; you couldn't hear anyone breathing. The people were thinking, *The minister can't even preach the sermon until the deacon does what he has to do.*

The elderly man reached Bill and paused. Then he dropped his cane on the floor and, with great difficulty, lowered himself and sat down next to Bill to worship with him.

The church was silent with emotion. When the minister gained control, he said, "What I am about to preach, you will never remember. What you have just seen, you will never forget."[8]

The story of the Good Samaritan and the story of the deacon and Bill are not only stories of compassion; they are also illustrations of salvation. The human race was helpless and hopeless in the grip of sin, untouched and uncared for, yet loved by God.

What that elderly deacon did for Bill is exactly what God has done for you and me. We were sitting all alone in our pain, shame, and righteous raggedness; and He sent His own Son down here to assure us that we need never be alone again. Jesus, in His compassion, is here. If we will allow Him, He will sit down beside us, and He will share His compassion with us and through us.

But You, O Lord, are a God full of compassion, and gracious,
Longsuffering and abundant in mercy and truth.

—PSALM 86:15

CHAPTER 6

A LIFE OF GENEROSITY

Generosity is not about what's in your bank
account—it's about what's in your heart.

"I want the last check I write to bounce."[1]

These are the words of billionaire philanthropist Charles F. Feeney, who made his fortune in the duty-free shopping industry and began secretly giving his money away in 1984. Feeney's goal was to make a difference in the world *while he was alive*. And he did. By 2016, he'd given more than $8 billion to charitable organizations around the world.

Feeney's "giving while you're living" philosophy did more than impact recipients; it also helped inspire Bill and Melinda Gates's charitable foundation. The other inspiration behind the Gates's philanthropy, according to Bill Gates, was his mother, Mary.

Gates often credits his journey toward generosity to a letter his mother sent his then-fiancée, Melinda, on the day before they were married. Mary reminded her son's bride that "from those to whom much is given, much is expected."[2]

Six months after writing that letter, Mary Gates died of breast cancer. After her death, Bill Gates, with his father's help, dedicated $100 million to what would become the Bill and Melinda Gates Foundation. From its inception, the foundation has given away more than $36 billion![3]

These are remarkable examples, of course. Not everyone has that kind of money to give. In fact, many of us view philanthropy as the work of the wealthy. After all, it's easy for them, right? They have plenty.

And that's where we've got it wrong. Extraordinary generosity is not a virtue reserved for the wealthy. In fact, it may be *easier* for those who have less to give more.

Take Albert Lexie, for example. In 1981, Albert started working at the Children's Hospital of Pittsburgh, cleaning and polishing shoes for $5 a pair. Satisfied customers often tipped him, usually a dollar or two. One Christmas, a customer gave Albert $50 for shining one pair of shoes! Big tips like that were rare, of course, and over the years, as styles changed, Albert saw his business dwindle.

In 2013, Albert retired after thirty-two years on the job. There was a farewell party. Hospital staff and administrators spoke of how much he'd be missed. But when he walked out the door on his last day, his influence at that hospital continued.

Why? Because during all those years of shining shoes, Albert Lexie donated more than 30 percent of his earnings to the hospital's Free Care Fund, which helps cash-strapped parents pay for their children's medical care. And those tips? He gave every single one to the hospital, more than $200,000 dollars in all.[4]

WHAT IS GENEROSITY?

Generosity is not about what's in your bank account—it's about what's in your heart. The word *generosity* is not found on our list of nine decisions that describe a life beyond amazing (Gal. 5:22–23). But the concept is there, hiding in the word *goodness*. Goodness is often misunderstood as the absence of evil. But in the Bible, goodness is not an *absence* of anything. It is the *presence* of something good.

We know that through the overflow of the heart, the mouth speaks. It is also true that through the overflow of the heart, we will act in one way or another. And if goodness is present in our hearts, that goodness will manifest itself in a generous spirit, in the words we say, and in the way we treat others.

The generous person gives others the benefit of the doubt and treats others with respect. She isn't worried about what the act of giving may cost in terms of time or effort. She doesn't wait to be asked and doesn't expect anything in return.

Most of us equate generosity with financial giving because that's what we hear about, that's what catches our attention. But generosity has a much fuller definition than that.

Respect, courtesy, forbearance, patience—all of these are expressions of a generous spirit. Each day you're given opportunities to exercise generosity of spirit: to respond to impatience with patience, to reply to a hurried or thoughtless comment with an expression of understanding or empathy, to overlook what you don't like in someone so you can seek and find what you do like.

This doesn't mean you tolerate everything that comes your way; it means you seek to understand first and react later. And the first part of understanding is remembering that we're all human and we're all in this together. Open your heart to generosity, and you'll be amazed at how God fills it.

For most of us, generosity doesn't come naturally. As children, we're fiercely protective of *our* toys. As teenagers we're more interested in fairness than benevolence. As adults, we're often so weighed down with financial worry we can find it difficult to be openhanded with what we have. But like every virtue in this book, generosity is one we can decide to cultivate, and we can depend on God to help us.

The apostle James said, "Every good gift and every perfect gift is from above, and comes down from the Father of lights, with whom there is no variation or shadow of turning" (James 1:17).

Our God is a generous God. Since we are made in His image, we can take comfort in knowing that generosity is within our reach. And "if ours is a world stamped from beginning to end by divine generosity, then it stands to reason that we ought to 'risk' a generosity of spirit commensurate to that reality!"[5]

LEARNING TO GIVE WHEN YOU DON'T HAVE MUCH

Generosity is a discipline that is more "caught" than taught. We understand it most when we see it in operation. Two of the best examples of generosity in action can be found in the New Testament. Both take place during the week before the crucifixion, burial, and resurrection of Jesus Christ.

In the first, we find Jesus sitting near the temple treasury, observing the people as they give their offerings (Mark 12:41–44).

There were thirteen receptacles in the temple where the Jews brought their taxes and tithes. Each treasury box had a large horn coming out of the top into which people placed their money, which then funneled down into the receptacle. Some worshipers deliberately made their offerings with many small coins so when they threw them into the brass horn, the sound could be heard all through the temple, echoing off the great stone walls.

On this particular day, Jesus watched many people cast in large amounts of money to be seen and heard by others. But then a poor widow came in and quietly made her meager offering.

In Greek (the language of the New Testament), the word we translate as "poor" is the word used to describe someone who is destitute—a pauper or a beggar.[6] In our day this widow might be someone depending on public assistance for survival or even someone who is homeless.

In spite of her poverty, this woman wanted to give. Some people avoid generosity because they have much and want to keep it all for themselves, while others hide behind having too little. This poor widow did not hide behind her poverty. Out of her love for God, she gave what she had.

In the book *God So Loved, He Gave*, Justin Borger wrote of his relationship with a homeless woman named Tammy:

> One of my jobs at church . . . was to fill out these small slips of paper that we gave Tammy and others to exchange for groceries at the local food bank. The only problem was that Tammy liked to share.
>
> "Don't give this away," I can remember telling her as I would hand her the slip for the food bank. "You need to keep this for yourself. Otherwise you'll run out and have nothing to eat." But after a while Tammy grew tired of being told not to share the

food that our church gave her. "I want to give some away too," she replied.

Living under the bridge meant living with other needy people, and so she let me know that it would be unthinkable for her to return there without sharing her groceries. "So, why can't I share some of it?" she asked with an incredulous stare. "Why can't I give some too?"

I found myself taken aback. *Why shouldn't Tammy be allowed to give some of what she'd received? Wasn't that exactly what I was doing?* I paused for a moment. But then I gave her a very pragmatic answer, telling her that our church deacons' fund wasn't set up for that. "We're giving this to *you*," I told Tammy, "not to everyone else you meet." Yet, I recognized the deeper problem: to only receive and never to give is to be belittled—to be humiliated. . . .

But the good news is that God has not only made us to be recipients of his grace but also participants in the movement of his own generosity. . . . He invites us—even the poorest of us (2 Cor. 8:1–3)—to live lives, however imperfectly, that extend and reflect his own role as Giver.[7]

In our story, Jesus tells us specifically what the poor widow gave: "two mites" (Mark 12:42). The word *mites* translates the Greek word *lepta*, the smallest denomination of coin minted in the Greek world. In the economy of that day, it was worth about 1/128th of one day's pay—not enough to buy a stale loaf of bread.

"That the widow places 'two' coins is significant," says Michael Card. "She could have kept one for herself. She does not."[8]

Never one to waste a teaching moment, Jesus said to His disciples, "This poor widow has put in more than all those who have given to the treasury; for they all put in out of their abundance, but she out of her poverty put in all that she had, her whole livelihood" (vv. 43–44).

You see, God's math defies everything we know about numbers. G. Campbell Morgan wrote:

> It is an amazing thing . . . He did not say, This poor woman hath done splendidly. He did not say, This poor woman hath cast in very much. He did not say, She hath cast in as much as anyone. He did not say, She hath cast in as much as the whole of them. He said, "More than all"! Presiding over the temple coffers that day, the Lord of the temple took the gifts and sifted them. On the one hand He put the gifts of wealth, and the gifts of ostentation; and on the other, two mite—"more than all"![9]

We should not read into this that all the wealthy donors of the day were evil. Surely some came with the right heart and gave for the right reasons—to honor God and contribute to the upkeep of the temple and the welfare of their community. But what Jesus saw that day was the opposite: He saw those who gave for show, motivated by pride and the desire to be recognized and applauded. In human terms, their gifts totaled more. But in God's sight, that total was less valuable than those two meager coins.

> Jesus indicated that the thing of most importance is not how much is given but the extent to which the gift is a sacrificial one. . . . A major element of Jesus' teaching is that attitude is more important than action. The widow's total giving demonstrates an attitude of absolute trust in God.[10]

When we give sacrificially, we're putting ourselves (from the world's perspective) in jeopardy. We're giving away what we need. But if we believe that God cares for us, that no good deed goes unnoticed by Him, and that He is endlessly rich in gifts, we'll be more inclined to reckless generosity.

Remember earlier in this chapter when I said it might actually be easier for those with less to be generous? The story of the widow's mite illustrates this truth. For some who are wealthy to casually give away a portion of their money is not a sacrifice, is it? But for the poor widow to give away "all that she had" is truly the epitome of generosity.

"Down through the ages those two minuscule coins have been multiplied into billions and billions for God's work as humble people have been liberated to give from their little. The Lord converted those two coins into a perennial wealth of contentment and instruction for his Church."[11]

EXTRAVAGANT GENEROSITY

Our second story takes place in the village of Bethany, the town where Jesus raised Lazarus from the dead. On this occasion a supper was hosted in the house of Simon the leper, no doubt a man Jesus had healed from leprosy, and Jesus was the guest of honor. Matthew, Mark, and John all record how, during dinner, a woman interrupted the proceedings in an act of generosity that may at first puzzle modern readers as much as it puzzled the disciples who witnessed it.

According to John's account, Lazarus's sister Mary, who could often be found sitting at Jesus' feet as He taught, "took a pound of very costly oil of spikenard, anointed the feet of Jesus, and wiped

His feet with her hair. And the house was filled with the fragrance of the oil" (John 12:3). The disciples murmured about the extravagance. One of them was so incensed that he spoke up:

> Judas Iscariot, Simon's son, who would betray Him, said, "Why was this fragrant oil not sold for three hundred denarii and given to the poor?" This he said, not that he cared for the poor, but because he was a thief, and had the money box; and he used to take what was put in it. (vv. 4–6)

In Jesus' day a denarius was one day's wages. Translated into modern terms, at a minimum wage of $10.50 per hour, one denarius would be $84. Three hundred denarii would be approximately $25,000. Put it like that, and we might be forgiven for wondering if Mary was out of her mind, pouring out $25,000 on someone's feet!

If you use human math, it's a shocking gesture. But remember, God's math defies everything we know about numbers. It may not make sense to us, but Jesus understood it, and it made sense to Him.

> "Leave her alone," said Jesus. "Why are you bothering her? She has done a beautiful thing to me. The poor you will always have with you, and you can help them any time you want. But you will not always have me. She did what she could. She poured perfume on my body beforehand to prepare for my burial. Truly I tell you, wherever the gospel is preached throughout the world, what she has done will also be told, in memory of her." (Mark 14:6–9 NIV)

Jesus knew the fate that awaited Him. What a gift it must have been for Him to experience the anointing that Mary gave; it was yet another sign that God would be with Him through the coming trials and torture.

Earlier we talked about having absolute trust in God to guide us in generosity. Mary had that trust. She trusted so completely that when she felt the Holy Spirit moving her to act in a supremely generous way, she did not hesitate.

The significance of this moment is captured in these words from noted Bible scholar Arno C. Gaebelein:

> Empires have risen, flourished, and passed away into the region of silence and oblivion. Monuments have been erected to commemorate human genius, greatness, and philanthropy—and these monuments have crumbled into the dust; but the act of this woman still lives, and shall live for ever. The hand of the Master has erected a monument to her, which shall never, no never, perish. May we have grace to imitate her.[12]

THE POTENTIAL OF A GENEROUS LIFE

By themselves, these two acts of radical, spontaneous generosity challenge our hearts. Then we see them against the backdrop of the culture in which they took place, and the impact is even greater.

In the Roman world, generosity was regarded as a virtue reserved for the rich and powerful. The Latin word *generosus,* which referred to a person's birth, comes from the Greek word *genesis,* which means "beginning." To be generous in the Roman world meant you had a good "beginning." Roman generosity was for the elite, the aristocrats. In fact, their culture depended on it. The wealthy acted as patrons, funding the work of artists and artisans, as well as commissioning public works. However, unlike our definition of generosity, which expects nothing in return, wealthy Roman citizens were compensated for the strain on their bank accounts. This could take the form of giving preferential business arrangements, promoting a patron for political office, advocating for laws favorable to the patron, or championing a benefactor's civil status.[13] (Come to think of it, it's not unlike America today!)

Neither Mary nor the widow who gave all that she had in the temple would have been expected to be generous. They were both swimming upstream against the culture and customs of their day.

As Americans, we like to pat ourselves on the back and repeat the mantra that we are the most generous nation in the world. Our government does give away a lot of money, but that does not make us a generous nation. Generous nations are made up of generous people, and it may shock you to learn that more than 85 percent of Americans give away less than 2 percent of their income.[14] And the numbers for evangelical Christians are not much better.

According to a recent study reported in *Relevant* magazine, only 10 to 25 percent of the people in a typical American congregation tithe (that is, give the biblical starting point of 10 percent) to the church, the poor, and kingdom causes. The same report concluded that if the remaining 75 to 90 percent of American Christians began to tithe regularly, global hunger, starvation, and death from preventable diseases could be relieved within five years. Additionally, illiteracy could all but be eliminated, the world's water and sanitation issues could be solved, all overseas mission work could be fully funded, and more than $100 billion per year would be left over for additional ministry.[15]

If this is true, why is generosity so hard? And how do we cultivate it in our lives? Let me share with you seven ways you can embrace and grow in generosity.

CHANGE THE WAY YOU THINK ABOUT MONEY

From the day we hold that first paycheck in our hands, we wonder, *What will I buy for myself?* We think of our wages as "ours." We earn our pay through our work, so it must belong to us. We bristle at the amount withheld for taxes, health care, and even our own retirement. We look at what we actually take home and allocate it to rent, bills, and daily necessities. And what's left? We'll protect that with the ferocity of a lion guarding its kill.

And now we're expected to just give some away to people or organizations who didn't work for it? That's a hard pill to swallow.

The most vital step we take toward developing a generous spirit is turning the way we think about money on its head. When we remember that "every good gift and every perfect gift is from above" (James 1:17), we realize that nothing good is really ours to start with. It's God's, and He bestows it on us as a gift to be used to glorify Him. When we start thinking of our money as just one of the countless good gifts from our Father who loves us, we can rest in the knowledge that He knows what we need, He promises to provide, and His storehouses are unending.

Think of it this way: You make a pie chart to see where your money's going. In this paradigm, the amount you have to work with is fixed, and each expenditure in every category takes away from the whole until you've used up the entire circle. It's a closed system. There's nothing for you outside that circle.

But God is infinite. He doesn't work in pie charts. He works in rivers. Rivers of blessings. And He never runs out.

If He is the one who supplies all our needs, and He never runs out of supplies, we can stop thinking about our money in terms of a pie being swiftly eaten up and start thinking of ourselves as conduits of His grace. What He gives to us, we can pass on to others without fear that there won't be enough left over for us.

EXPOSE YOUR HEART TO THE BROKENNESS OF HUMANITY

Living in a prosperous nation with a welfare system that, though flawed, does provide a safety net of sorts to needy people, it's easy to think that everyone has what they need. But that's not the case. And if there's poverty in one of the wealthiest countries in the world, how much more is there in the poorest countries?

At the beginning of this chapter you learned that two people—his mother, Mary, and a philanthropist named Charles Feeney—influenced Bill Gates to give away a large portion of his vast fortune. But there's more to the story.

According to his wife, Melinda, while Bill was visiting a hospital in Africa that treated tuberculosis patients, he called her while "quite choked up." He'd just seen firsthand how awful it was to have tuberculosis. "It's a death sentence," he said. "To go into that hospital is a death sentence." From that moment on, Bill Gates was not content to donate money to that one hospital. He wanted to do things that could help "thousands and millions get out of poverty altogether."[16]

Several years ago, four hundred members of our congregation went to Swaziland, Africa, to help people in that impoverished country plant crops. We were there for ten days, and none of us will ever forget it.

Swaziland is a desperately poor country, and at that time it had the highest per capita rate of AIDS in the world. We went to serve and to grow in understanding, and we were given that opportunity in small ways and in profound, unforgettable ways—one of our members sat in a hut and held a man as he died of AIDS.

Late one afternoon, one of the trip's organizers asked me to speak to the pastors. While most of the pastors spoke and understood English, many didn't read or write. Often, they had only a portion of a Bible, not even a complete one. Yet somehow, with all the technology we have, our ministry had touched them.

One of the pastors came up to me and told me how he and the other pastors gathered each week to hear a broadcast of my sermons on an old radio—the only way they could hear them.

"I listen to you every Sunday morning," he told me. "And then I go tell my people what you said."

I started to cry.

What did we hope to do in Swaziland? We hoped to do what Jesus calls us to do, to care for each other. We did not expect our presence to fix everything, and we did not overestimate our worth to them. But there is no way to express their worth to us. The people we met changed our lives because they changed our hearts.

My wife joined us on that trip. We had been told to bring large supplies of little gifts to give to the hundreds of children we would meet along the way. I couldn't believe the number of bracelets and necklaces my wife packed into one suitcase. She was determined to have enough to last the entire trip. But when she saw the poverty of those precious children and heard their voices and saw their outstretched hands, she gave everything away within the first two days. She could not bear to say no to even one of them.

Until you see and know the plight of the needy, you will never give to them. Once you do, you'll never be able to stop! And you don't have to travel halfway across the world to understand the plight of the poor. They are in every American city and across rural

America. Chances are good that you work or worship with many people who are just getting by, who live paycheck to paycheck, and are one unexpected expense away from not being able to put food on the table.

BEFORE YOU DO THE BIG THINGS, DO THE LITTLE THINGS

We won't automatically become generous in a day. But we can begin to do little things we thought were unimportant.

- Consciously increase the amount you leave on the table for the waiter or waitress who serves you in restaurants. (Remember what Albert was able to do with his tips!)
- Carry some money with you specifically to give away to someone in need, and ask God to reveal ways to express love and generosity to the people you meet every day.
- Make a commitment to support your church and discover the joy and impact of tithing.

I received this letter from one of the grandmothers in our congregation:

Dear Pastor,

Since you are a grandpa, I'm sure you appreciate stories of generosity showing up in your grandchildren. I want to share one with you concerning my youngest grandson, who is 8 years old. His Awana club adopted a group of poor children in Turkmenistan. Each child in the club was given a jar in which they could place quarters to save up for other children.

One day, my son saw that his son had put a five-dollar bill (his entire monthly allowance) in his jar. When my son asked him why he did that, my grandson replied, "I want the children to hear about Jesus. Anyway, I would just buy another toy with the money." This touched my heart so much, and continues to make me think about what "toy" I could forego in order to spread the gospel.

We develop a habit of generosity in the same way we develop any good habit, through incremental adjustments we can maintain over the long haul. It's far better to start small and build up from there than to make one huge gift to a church or charity and fall into complacency because we've "done our part."

Generosity isn't a "one-and-done" situation. It's a lifestyle.

START GIVING MORE THAN YOU CAN AFFORD

The next step after giving a little is giving a lot. In one of his letters to the believers in Corinth, Paul reported on the generosity of Christians living in Macedonia.

Now I want you to know, dear brothers and sisters, what God in his kindness has done through the churches in Macedonia. They are being tested by many troubles, and they are very poor. But they are also filled with abundant joy, which has overflowed in rich generosity.

For I can testify that they gave not only what they could afford, but far more. And they did it of their own free will. They begged us again and again for the privilege of sharing in the gift for the believers in Jerusalem. (2 Cor. 8:1–4 NLT)

Just like the poor widow, these believers gave not out of their abundance but out of their poverty. And they weren't content to give only a little. They wanted to give all that they had—and more.

At this point you might be asking, "Just how much should I give?" Especially if you are someone who budgets and tracks your expenses, you may want a hard-and-fast rule, a percentage. You want to know how big a piece of the pie this generosity will require. In his best-known book, *Mere Christianity*, C. S. Lewis tried to answer that question:

> I do not believe one can settle how much we ought to give. I am afraid the only safe way is to give more than we can spare. In other words, if our expenditure on comforts, luxuries, amusements, etc., is up to the standard common among those with the same income as our own, we are probably giving away too little. If our charities do not at all pinch or hamper us, I should say they [our expenditures] are too small. There ought to be things we should like to do and cannot do because our charities expenditure excludes them.[17]

The answer to the question "How much should I give?" is then "More than you can afford." We all spend far more on things we don't need than on the causes that are truly close to God's heart, namely, the spread of the gospel and the care of the poor.

DON'T BE AFRAID OF SPONTANEITY

All of us have experienced the awkwardness of the long red light that extends the encounter with the homeless person on the corner.

We try to look past her, and we pray for the light to change. In a similar fashion, we keep our eyes fixed doggedly on the door of the convenience store to avoid eye contact with the person sitting on the curb by the entrance, knowing that if he sees us notice him, he will ask us for money. We tell ourselves that obviously we can't help *everyone*. But we should never let that allow us to conclude that we should not try to help *anyone*.

Several months ago my wife, Donna, came upon a mother with two little girls who was standing in front of a business, asking for help. At first she drove past them. But she knew in her heart she was supposed to help them, so she went to a nearby pizzeria and bought a pizza. When she returned, she handed the woman some money and gave the pizza to the little girls. When she told me later what happened next, she choked up. "I have never seen two little girls so hungry and so excited to get a pizza."

God didn't create the world and then leave us to our own devices. He is always interested, always involved, and always putting us just where He wants us in order to carry out His work on earth. What can seem like a chance meeting or a moment of spontaneity to us is all part of His plan—and no act of generosity is too small.

Weekly, perhaps daily, we pass people in need, not only street people and those who have fallen on hard times, but others. As adults, we know that if we stop to help everyone, we'll never get anything done. But that doesn't mean we never stop. It means we use discernment and judgment, and we put our faith in the Holy Spirit to move us to act. And then . . . we act.

If you have the attitude to help others, the Lord will show you what to do. Ask God every day—every single day—to make you sensitive to the people you should help. And He will.

PRAY ABOUT BECOMING A RADICAL

Have you ever considered our Lord's radical generosity toward you?

"For you know the grace of our Lord Jesus Christ, that though He was rich, yet for your sakes He became poor, that you through His poverty might become rich" (2 Cor. 8:9).

Radical generosity is the giving of all your "time, talent, and treasures for the sake of God's kingdom and a heavenly reward, without expecting any (earthly) return on investment."[18]

What does a life of radical generosity look like?

Consider David Green, the founder of Hobby Lobby. Today Green is worth an estimated $5.8 billion—the eighty-first richest man in America, according to *Forbes*. But Green's story of generosity began in his garage in 1970, when he and his wife, Barbara, began making picture frames. After many years of dreaming and hard work, they turned their initial plan into the largest privately owned arts-and-craft retailer in the world. Today Hobby Lobby does $4 billion in yearly sales and employs more than thirty thousand people in forty-seven states.

Each year Green and his family give away 50 percent of the company's profits. It is estimated that he has given away upwards of $500 million in his lifetime, buying and donating land and properties to a variety of ministries around the world. He also has helped fund the worldwide delivery of more than 1.4 billion copies of gospel literature.

The driving force behind Green's generosity is a vision of something bigger than this life: "I want to know that I have affected people for eternity. I believe I am. I believe once someone knows Christ as their personal savior, I've affected eternity. I matter 10 billion years from now."[19]

Remember Charles Feeney, the billionaire philanthropist who inspired Bill and Melinda Gates? He made a fortune and then grew it larger by investing wisely—so that he could give more money away. In fact, he may have given away a greater portion of his wealth than any major American philanthropist of our day.

But Charles Feeney has never owned a house or a car. Until he was seventy-five, he traveled in coach, not first class. He wears simple clothes, an inexpensive plastic watch, and prefers the hamburgers at his favorite local restaurant to fine dining.

At the end of 2016, Charles Feeney's foundation gave away its last $7 million—to Cornell University to help students serve their community.[20] He may not have bounced a check yet, but he's certainly met his goal of "giving while living."

MAKE SURE YOU'RE MOVING TOWARD YOUR TREASURE

Many people are familiar with the following words of Jesus:

> "Do not lay up for yourselves treasures on earth, where moth and rust destroy and where thieves break in and steal; but lay up for yourselves treasures in heaven, where neither moth nor rust destroys and where thieves do not break in and steal. For where your treasure is, there your heart will be also." (Matt. 6:19–21)

Far fewer of us are intimately familiar with these wise words from the apostle Paul:

> Teach those who are rich in this world not to be proud and not to trust in their money, which is so unreliable. Their trust should

be in God, who richly gives us all we need for our enjoyment. Tell them to use their money to do good. They should be rich in good works and generous to those in need, always being ready to share with others. By doing this they will be storing up their treasure as a good foundation for the future so that they may experience true life. (1 Tim. 6:17–19 NLT)

You may not think of yourself as rich, but you are. According to *Forbes*, "The typical person in the bottom 5 percent of the American income distribution is still richer than 68 percent of the world's inhabitants."[21]

No matter what your income, you are either moving away from your treasure or toward it. The Lord Jesus gives us a choice in the matter. Every heartbeat brings us one moment closer to eternity. If we selfishly spend our lives in the pursuit of wealth on earth, then we waste our lives. But if your treasure is in heaven, you are always moving toward it.

In many cultures throughout history, the dead were buried with items they might need in the next life. Think of the lavish tombs of the Egyptian pharaohs, stuffed with gold, precious jewels, weapons, and even food! Or the vast underground army of terracotta soldiers buried with Qin Shi Huang, China's first emperor, meant to protect him in the afterlife. But no matter who we are or how much we amass on this earth, none of it follows us when we die.

Bestselling author Stephen King shared these words with the 2001 graduating class at Vassar College:

A couple of years ago, I found out what "you can't take it with you" means. I found out while I was lying in a ditch at the side of a country road, covered with mud and blood and with the tibia of my right leg poking out of the side of my jeans like the branch of a tree taken down in a thunderstorm. I had a MasterCard in my wallet, but when you're lying in the ditch with broken glass in your hair, no one accepts MasterCard.

We come in naked and broke. We may be dressed when we go out, but we're just as broke. Warren Buffet? Going to go out broke. Bill Gates? Going out broke. Tom Hanks? Going out broke. Steve King? Broke. Not a crying dime.

All the money you earn, all the stocks you buy, all the mutual funds you trade—all of that is mostly smoke and mirrors. It's still going to be a quarter past getting late whether you tell the time on a Timex or a Rolex. . . .

So I want you to consider making your life one long gift to others. And why not? All you have is on loan, anyway. All that lasts is what you pass on. . . .

[This needy world is] not a pretty picture, but we have the power to help, the power to change. And why should we refuse? Because we're going to take it with us? Please. . . .

A life of giving—not just money, but time and spirit—repays. It helps us remember that we may be going out broke, but right now we're doing okay. Right now we have the power to do great good for others and for ourselves.

So I ask you to begin giving, and to continue as you begin. I think you'll find in the end that you got more than you ever had, and did more good than you ever dreamed.[22]

Several years ago a video was posted online of a woman selling roses on a New York City subway train for $1 each. In the video, a man approaches her and asks how much for all the roses she has to sell. He gives her $140 for the entire bunch, but instead of taking his purchase with him, he asks the rose vendor to give them away to other people. When the train stops, he steps off, leaving the woman utterly stunned. She begins to sob.

Maria Lopez, the bystander who filmed the encounter, told the *Huffington Post*: "She started crying from the relief of someone actually being generous. This one little gesture of humanity is so huge. It's a testament to the lack of love and lack of generosity in the world. I think people are yearning for that."[23]

Yes, people are yearning for it. And with your every spontaneous act of generosity, you are giving others the hope they may have been on the cusp of abandoning. God puts you where He wants you so that you will take advantage of opportunities to love and give.

Remember what we learned at the beginning of this chapter: Generosity isn't about dollar signs. It's about the heart. It's about holding the gifts of God in an open hand rather than clenching our fists around them and holding on for dear life.

Whether you're the next Bill Gates or you live balanced on the razor's edge of poverty, you have the opportunity to change the world through generosity. God's economy does not fit within our pie charts. It's so much bigger and better and more benevolent than that. And we've been given the unsurpassable gift of being His hands and feet, of being the conduits of His love in a world that desperately needs it.

I am praying that you will put into action the generosity
that comes from your faith as you understand and
experience all the good things we have in Christ.

—PHILEMON 1:6 NLT

CHAPTER 7

A LIFE OF INTEGRITY

Integrity is telling the truth to yourself.
Honesty is telling the truth to others.

Nineteen-year-old Joey Prusak was on duty at the Dairy Queen counter in Hopkins, Minnesota, when a blind man placed an order. As the man paid, a twenty-dollar bill slipped from his pocket and fell to the floor. The woman behind him quickly snatched up the bill and stuffed it into her purse. When she stepped up to the counter, Joey asked her to return the money to the blind man. She refused, claiming she dropped the bill herself. Joey knew better, and when she still refused after his second request, he declined to serve her and told her to leave the store. He remained calm as the woman blasted him with an angry tirade and stormed out the door.

Joey went directly to the table where the man was eating, explained what had happened, and gave him a twenty from his own billfold. A customer who witnessed the scene e-mailed an account of it to Dairy Queen. The store posted the e-mail, someone photographed it, and put it on Facebook, and the story went viral. It was soon reported on newscasts and in newspapers across the nation, and Joey was inundated with calls and accolades. He even got a call from Warren Buffet, whose company owns Dairy Queen, thanking him and inviting him to the next shareholders meeting.[1]

Why did this teenager's heartwarming deed draw so much attention? Because while we live in a world where cutting moral corners is the norm, our hearts know we were made for better. We long for a world in which integrity is our way of life, and deeds like Joey's are the norm.

We may not see that world in our lifetimes, but we can create that world within ourselves. That's what we do when we strive to live with integrity. Stories like this remind us that if a nineteen-year-old working at a Dairy Queen can live with such integrity, we can too. In these troubled times, that's deeply reassuring.

There have always been people who boast about "getting away with it," who cut moral corners, or believe the rules don't apply to them. But today it's different. Popular culture celebrates such people; and today's technology constantly parades them in front of our eyes, discouraging our efforts to live more truthfully.

In 2012, successful businesswoman and investor Amy Rees Anderson wrote a short article in *Forbes* magazine, "Success Will Come and Go, but Integrity Is Forever," about whether integrity still matters. Here's her assessment:

> We live in a world where integrity isn't talked about nearly enough. We live in a world where "the end justifies the means" has become an acceptable school of thought for far too many.

Sales people overpromise and under deliver, all in the name of making their quota for the month. Applicants exaggerate in job interviews because they desperately need a job. CEOs overstate projected earnings because they don't want the board of directors to replace them. . . . Customer service representatives cover up a mistake they made because they're afraid the client will leave them. Employees call in "sick" because they don't have any more paid time off when they actually just need to get their Christmas shopping done. The list could go on and on, and in each case the person committing the act of dishonesty tells themselves they had a perfectly valid reason why the end result justified their lack of integrity.[2]

Integrity starts with what we tell ourselves. When we cut moral corners, there's always one person who knows the truth—the person looking back at us in the mirror every morning. Sure, we can lie to ourselves, rationalize, make excuses, or deny. But when we do, what we're really denying and running away from is the truth of who God is: He knows everything we do, think, and feel. Lying to ourselves may let us justify what we've done, but it never fools God.

The *Oxford Dictionary* defines *integrity* as "the quality of being honest and having strong moral principles." Synonyms include *honesty, honor, good character, fairness, sincerity,* and *trustworthiness*— all virtues of a Christian life.

But if we read further, the dictionary's second definition of integrity gives us a deeper insight: "the state of being whole and undivided."[3]

Whole and undivided. To have integrity is to feel complete, to have all parts of your life integrated; to have them intact, interconnected, uncorrupted, and operating together as a single unit.

A person of integrity has it so deeply woven into his character that it's integrated into his innermost being as a consistent standard from which all his actions flow. Such a person amazes us. Such a person is who we want to be.

THE FAITHFULNESS OF GOD

The biblical term for *integrity* is "faithfulness." And faithfulness is one of the key attributes of God.

As you open the pages of the Old Testament, you're introduced to the faithful God almost immediately. One day Moses came to God and asked for His name. And God said to Moses, "I AM WHO I AM" (Ex. 3:14).

That seems like a strange way to respond to Moses' question, but what God was saying was this: "I am the God who has no past and no future. I am the God of the eternal present. I am the faithful God, and what I say is true." In the mind and heart of God, the promise and fulfillment are viewed in the same tense. God does not look to be faithful in the future. God is always faithful because God lives in the eternal now.

Do you remember the insurance company commercial that used the image of a gigantic rock to demonstrate stability? They asked you to "get a piece of the rock," implying that if you bought this kind of insurance, you could be sure it would be there when you needed it.

That ad struck a chord because we want immovable, unbreakable strength and protection, like that of a giant boulder, securing us in life. Our souls crave the rocklike strength of a character formed in the image of God. And we can have it, because the stability of people with this kind of moral fiber is rooted in their integrity.

Deuteronomy 32:4 says, "He [God] is the Rock, His work is perfect; for all His ways are justice, a God of truth and without injustice; righteous and upright is He."

Integrity isn't always easy, but it is deeply rewarding and reassuring. If you've lived a life of taking moral shortcuts, you carry a heavy burden. That burden weighs on you, pushing you further and further down to moral decay.

You must renounce your dishonesty, repent to God, ask forgiveness, and make amends whenever you can. If you truly aspire to rock-solid integrity, sincerely ask the Holy Spirit for the strength to change and give your all to make that change happen. When you do this, the faithfulness and integrity of God will begin to flow into your life.

WHAT IS INTEGRITY?

In his book *The Seven Habits of Highly Effective People*, Stephen Covey says integrity is

> the value we place on ourselves. It's our ability to make and keep commitments to ourselves, to "walk our talk." . . . Your discipline comes from within; it's a function of your independent will. You are a disciple, a follower of your own deep values and their source. And you have the will, the integrity to subordinate your feelings, your impulses, your moods to those values.[4]

Sometimes described as fidelity, sometimes as steadfastness, integrity always means the determination to stand by your word and complete your commitment. A person of integrity is consistently faithful to the truth, committed to doing the right thing, and does what he says he will do.

This faithfulness is not just an important truth about God, it's an important theme in the Bible. The word itself appears twenty-one times, most often in the book of Proverbs. The superior example of integrity in the Bible is Job. Joseph and Daniel are also especially marked by this trait.

The writer of the book of Proverbs asks, "A faithful man who can find?" (20:6 KJV). And throughout the entirety of the Bible we are given the answer to that question: not so many. In the Old Testament, only five are given the title of "faithful": Daniel, Hanani, Moses, Samuel, and Abraham.

In the New Testament, only eight—Lydia, Timothy, Paul, Tychicus, Epaphrus, Onesimus, Silvanus, and Antipas—were declared "faithful" people.

Do you recognize all of those names? Probably not. In this list of faithful people from the Bible, there are more obscure personalities than well-known ones. But whether they're less-known, like Hanani and Epaphrus, or familiar, like Abraham and Paul, they're all honored today, millenia later, for their integrity. What matters to God isn't how important, how well-known, or how talented they were. What matters to Him is how faithful they were!

Integrity isn't reserved for what our culture perceives as "greatness" or "importance." It's honored by God among all of us—those who live quietly humble lives, those who suffer, and those whom society assumes will be forgotten, as well as those whose names we all know. Pastor Rick Ezell wrote:

Integrity is not reputation—others' opinion of us. Integrity is not success—our accomplishments. Integrity embodies the sum total of our being and our actions. Integrity is not something we have, but something we are. It inevitably shows itself in what we do and say. Integrity is needed because people are watching us. Will our behavior match our beliefs? Will our character correspond with our confession?[5]

People like this are honest in their business dealings. They avoid slander and gossip. They keep confidences and don't falsely impugn the integrity or motives of others. They speak respectfully and appropriately and treat others well—even those they don't know. They're willing to say, "I was wrong," and take responsibility for their own errors—even those that could have been hidden or blamed on others. To paraphrase Will Rogers, "They live in such a way that they wouldn't be ashamed to sell the family parrot to the town gossip."[6]

Warren Buffet, chairman and CEO of Berkshire Hathaway, described the significance of integrity when he said: "We look for three things when we hire people. We look for intelligence, we look for initiative or energy, and we look for integrity. And if they don't have the latter, the first two will kill you."[7]

Now that we have a pretty good handle on its meaning, let's look at several decisions you can make to become a person of integrity.

BE HONEST WITH YOURSELF

Before you begin your journey toward integrity, you need to determine your starting point. In other words, what's your integrity quotient? How much integrity do you have?

In his book *Honesty, Morality, and Conscience*, Jerry White told the following story about the legendary baseball player Ted Williams:

When Ted Williams was forty years old and closing out his career with the Boston Red Sox, he was suffering from a pinched nerve in his neck. "The thing was so bad," he later explained, "that I could hardly turn my head to look at the pitcher." . . . For the first time in his career he batted under .300, hitting just .254 with 10 home runs. He was the highest salaried player in sports that year, making $125,000. The next year the Red Sox sent him the same contract.

"When I got it, I sent it back with a note. I told them I wouldn't sign it until they gave me the full pay cut allowed. I think it was 25 percent. My feeling was that I was always treated fairly by the Red Sox when it came to contracts.

"I never had any problem with them about money. Now they were offering me a contract I didn't deserve. And I only wanted what I deserved." . . .

Williams cut his own salary by $31,250![8]

As believers we need to be ruthlessly honest with ourselves. "Of all the lies we tell, the ones we tell ourselves are the most deadly. Question your motives. Stop justifying what you know to be wrong. Stop excusing yourself."[9]

David once asked God to help him with this, and here from Psalm 139 is his honest prayer:

> O Lord, you have examined my heart
>   and know everything about me.
> You know when I sit down or stand up.
>   You know my thoughts even when I'm far away.
>
> Search me, O God, and know my heart;
>   test me and know my anxious thoughts.

Point out anything in me that offends you,
and lead me along the path of everlasting life.

(vv. 1–2, 23–24 NLT)

Do a moral inventory of yourself. Hold yourself accountable going forward for what you say and do. Moving toward a more faithful, fair, and honest life begins with confronting truthfully who you are. You can't hold yourself accountable if you won't see yourself clearly.

I truly wish I could give you an easier place to start, but I can't. Let me tell you what I know: You can't go anywhere if you don't start from the truth. Confession basically means saying the same thing about your sin as God says. So if you say you want to develop integrity, but you're not willing to face the rough parts and confess them, you won't get there.

TELL THE TRUTH

One way integrity reveals itself is by speaking the truth. Take note of a couple of proverbs:

The integrity of the upright will guide them,
But the perversity of the unfaithful will destroy them.
(Prov. 11:3)

Lying lips are an abomination to the LORD,
But those who deal truthfully are His delight. (Prov. 12:22)

We reflect God's character when we speak the truth, for "God . . . does not lie" (Titus 1:2 NIV). But this is not easy:

Honesty has always been hard to find. Diogenes, the Greek philosopher, lit a candle in the daytime and traveled about looking for an honest person. Blaise Pascal said he didn't expect to meet three honest men in a century. . . .

Honesty is like a boomerang. Our words, along with who we are, always travel full circle. Every time individuals engage in dishonest activities of any kind the results come back to haunt them. Just ask any politician about skeletons in the closet.[10]

When we always speak the truth, we don't have to look back over our shoulders with fear. We're not always "covering our tracks." Speaking the truth is at the core of integrity. Once again the writer of Proverbs says, "He who walks with integrity walks securely, but he who perverts his ways will become known" (10:9).

This is not a license to say unkind things because you believe them to be true. Never forget that with genuine integrity comes spiritual maturity and grace. Jesus was full of grace and truth. He wasn't bashful about speaking the truth. When He spoke the truth, it was out of love for us.

We all know people who are full of much grace but no truth. They're nice and warm and fuzzy, but there's no real truth in them. On the other hand, we also know people who have truth without grace and, well . . . no one really wants to listen to them!

Believe it or not, speaking the truth is a character trait Christian leaders need to work on. For example, a favorite indoor sport of many pastors is the embellishment of church attendance. We call it "speaking evangelistically."

I heard about two pastors who were talking about their church attendance. One pastor said to the other, "If I lie about my attendances, and you know that I am lying about my attendances, and I know that you know that I am lying about my attendances, isn't that like telling the truth?"

On the other hand, there are those who speak the truth about their numbers. Someone asked another pastor about his attendance with this inquiry: "Pastor, what are you running this year in your church?" To which the pastor honestly replied, "We are running over one thousand, but we are catching only about six hundred."

KEEP YOUR WORD

Before leaving Mount Vernon to assume the presidency, in the spring of 1789, George Washington wrote: "Integrity & firmness is all I can promise—these, be the voyage long or short; never shall forsake me although I may be deserted by all men."[11]

Washington was surrounded by brilliant men: Benjamin Franklin, Thomas Jefferson, Patrick Henry, John Adams, Alexander Hamilton, James Madison, and more. Almost all of them were better educated than he was, and certainly many were ambitious; some even became presidents. But at three different junctures during the war for independence and the founding of our country, three times when everything hung in the balance, all these brilliant, well-educated men chose George Washington as their leader. Why?

What was it about Washington that consistently earned him his peers' highest trust and admiration? In the writings of his contemporaries and of historians who have studied his life, one reason is mentioned more frequently than any other: "The most commonly cited characteristic given for his emergence as the supreme leader is his character."[12]

They trusted him to keep his word because he always had.

On more than one occasion, Washington could have changed the course of history by becoming more monarch than president, by enriching himself instead of tending to the welfare of the young country, and by gathering and keeping power when it was time for him to step down. But instead, he kept his word.

Keeping your word is a cornerstone to integrity, and people around you will know it and respect it. As we noted earlier, integrity means all parts of your character are unified by faithfulness to truth. Breaking your word breaks that unity, and the shattered pieces of character fall away like shards of broken pottery.

In Robert Bolt's play *A Man for All Seasons*, Thomas More says, "When a man takes an oath . . . he's holding his own self in his own hands. Like water. And if he opens his fingers *then*—he needn't hope to find himself again."[13]

If I've made a promise, then I have no alternative but to keep it, whether I've promised a small thing like picking up the cleaning or a large one like a Mediterranean cruise. I must do what I say I will do for no other reason than that I said I would do it. Otherwise, my integrity is at stake. Are there things beyond my control that can prevent me from keeping my word? Yes, but it's still my responsibility to do what I can, and to be certain the interruption or event wasn't partly caused because I failed to do all I could to keep my word.

The person who keeps his promises reflects the character of God. "Know that the LORD your God, He is God, the faithful God who keeps covenant and mercy for a thousand generations with those who love Him and keep His commandments" (Deut. 7:9).

Here's another definition of integrity that takes this particular point to the edge: Integrity is keeping a commitment after the circumstances under which the commitment was made have changed.

A store owner interviewed a young man for a job. He asked, "If

I hire you to work in my store, will you be honest and truthful?" The young man answered, "I will be honest and truthful whether you hire me or not."

BE WHO YOU ARE

Many years ago I heard a Southern preacher give this word of wisdom about integrity: "Be what you is, not what you ain't; 'cause if you ain't what you is, you is what you ain't." To live with integrity means you live a genuine and sincere life. You are the same person no matter the circumstances.

Paul instructed the Philippians: "Be sincere and without offense till the day of Christ" (Phil. 1:10). Let's take a closer look at the word *sincere* that Paul used here:

> One synonym for *integrity* is *sincerity*—the state of being truthful, genuine, and free of deception or duplicity. The word *sincerity* comes from the Latin *sincerus*, meaning "clean and pure through and through." The Latin *sincerus* comes from two Latin root words, *sine* ("without") and *cera* ("wax"). Tradition tells us dishonest Roman sculptors would cover up nicks and flaws in their statues with a wax filler. The deception would last only until a hot summer sun melted the wax and exposed the flaw. A sculpture that was pure and flawless was said to be *sine cera*, without wax.
>
> In the same way, a human life that is pure and whole is *sine cera*, without wax.[14]

Of all the questions people ask my family and friends about me, these are at the top of the list: What's Dr. Jeremiah like at home? What's he like with his children? With his wife? What's he like backstage before he walks out to speak?

What they are asking is: Is he a man of integrity? I pray the answer to that question will always be positive! A person of integrity will not be a respectable Dr. Jekyll at work who morphs into a raging Mr. Hyde at home.

In the ancient Greek theater, actors wore masks molded or painted with set expressions designed to reflect their character's persona. These actors were called hypocrites, which at the time meant "actor"—one who takes on the personality of a scripted character in a staged story. In time, the word *hypocrite* was applied metaphorically to anyone who pretends to be something he's not, especially with intent to deceive.

Authentic people don't wear masks to hide who they are. They don't adjust their personae or modify their standards to fit whatever group or situation they're in. They're the same people, acting by the same standard, wherever they are. The "you" at church should be the same as the "you" at home, at work, while driving, when on the Internet, or when posting on Facebook or Twitter.

John Wesley was once asked by a woman what he would do if he knew that at midnight the next night he would die. After he thought about it for a minute, he said, "Well, I would do just what I intend to do. I would preach at Gloucester this evening, and again at five o'clock tomorrow morning. I would ride to Tewkesbury and preach in the afternoon and I would meet the societies after the meeting. I would go to Martin's who has invited me over for entertainment, and I would retire at ten o'clock. I would commend myself to my Heavenly Father, lie down to rest, and wake up in glory."[15]

He was saying that if he knew he would die tomorrow night, he wouldn't have to change anything because he had determined to be faithful to what God had called him to do.

The Lord our God, He is one. If we strive to be like Him, whole to the core, our lives will become simpler and less complicated. Just as God is one, my goal as a person is to be one. Find the center of who you are and be that.

AVOID BAD COMPANY

The apostle Paul said, "Bad company corrupts good character" (1 Cor. 15:33 NLT).

We think we know the people around us, but the ability to discern the truth in others is rarer than you might think. I've had people in my office whom I've sat and talked with and counseled and yet have not been certain whether they're speaking the truth or not.

Discernment is something we continue to grow in throughout our lives, but there are some behaviors that are unmistakable. I'm always surprised at how many good people rationalize to themselves the behavior of those around them, or say they failed to see red flags. Did they really? Or did they just not want to see them?

Just as you can speak the truth to yourself about your own behavior if you choose to, you can also speak the truth to yourself about the behavior of others *if you choose to*.

Don't underestimate the influence on you of those you associate with. If their behavior is positive, you'll feel uplifted. If being around them leaves you drained of joy and positivity, if you're uncomfortable, depressed, hurt, or scared in their presence, then you have your answer.

Negativity is corrosive. Negative behavior is contagious.

Sometimes we really do miss those red flags. If you feel you truly can't discern the character of those around you, ask the Holy Spirit to reveal it you. And listen to what He puts in your heart!

Amy Rees Anderson has given us this piece of advice:

Avoid those who are not trustworthy. Do not do business with them. Do not associate with them. Do not make excuses for them. Do not allow yourself to get enticed into believing that "while they may be dishonest with others, they would never be dishonest with me." If someone is dishonest in any aspect of his life you can be guaranteed he will be dishonest in many aspects of his life. You cannot dismiss even those little acts of dishonesty, such as the person who takes two newspapers from the stand when they paid for only one. After all, if a person cannot be trusted in the simplest matters of honesty then how can they possibly be trusted to uphold lengthy and complex business contracts? . . .

"When you lie down with dogs you get fleas." Inevitably we become more and more like the people we surround ourselves with day to day. If we surround ourselves with people who are dishonest and willing to cut corners to get ahead, then we'll surely find ourselves following a pattern of first enduring their behavior, then accepting their behavior, and finally adopting their behavior. If you want to build a reputation as a person of integrity then surround yourself with people of integrity.[16]

BE FOUND FAITHFUL

One of the great verses on integrity is 1 Corinthians 4:2: "Moreover it is required in stewards that one be found faithful."

A steward is someone who manages the affairs of another.

A steward's success is determined by whether or not he has been faithful, trustworthy, and dependable in carrying out his assignment. So how does God determine if we have been faithful to Him?

> Paul answered this question when he wrote, "Moreover it is required in stewards that one be *found* faithful." The word "found" is the translation of a Greek word that describes a discovery made as a result of careful observance. It tells us that God is carefully watching us to see our actions and reactions. He is watching how we treat people, how we respond to pressure, and whether or not we have the tenacity to stay on track when distractions try to thwart our obedience.
>
> Integrity means exercising trustworthy behavior over a long period of time. Faithful people have proven they can be trusted for the long haul. You don't have to check up on them. You don't have to worry that, even if they did a good job last week, they might let you down this week. No, faithful people show that they are routinely dependable in all kinds of ways and all kinds of circumstances. Faithfulness is the character of somebody you know you can rely on all the time.[17]

Os Guinness grew up in China, a country that had been ravaged by two centuries of foreign adventuring, World War II, and a brutal civil war. He lived with his parents in Nanjing, the nation's capital at the time. The city had few good English-language schools, so at the age of five he was sent off by plane to a boarding school in Shanghai. He wrote:

> Obviously, the conditions behind the decision to send me out at that age were extreme, and I was not the only one launched

on that path so young. But it was the first time in my life that I had been away from my parents and on my own. So, to give me a constant reminder of the North Star of the faith at the center of our family life, my father had searched for two small, smooth, flat stones and painted on them his life motto and that of my mother. For many years those two little stones were tangible memos in the pockets of my gray flannel shorts that were the uniform of most English schoolboys in those days. In my right-hand pocket was my father's motto, "Found Faithful," and in my left-hand pocket was my mother's, "Please Him."

Many years have passed since then, and both those little painted stones were lost in the chaos of escaping from China when Mao Zedong and the People's Army eventually overran Nanjing, returned the capital to Beijing and began their iron and bloody rule of the entire country. But I have never forgotten the lesson of the little stones. Followers of Jesus are called to be "found faithful" and to "please him," always, everywhere and in spite of everyone and everything.[18]

One of the most powerful statements of integrity in the Bible is found in the Old Testament book of Habakkuk. After the prophet had grappled with God over some very difficult issues, he came to this conclusion:

Even though the fig trees have no blossoms, and there are no grapes on the vines; even though the olive crop fails, and the fields lie empty and barren; even though the flocks die in the fields, and the cattle barns are empty, yet I will rejoice in the LORD! I will be joyful in the God of my salvation! (Hab. 3:17–18 NLT)

BE STRONG UNDER FIRE

The book of Daniel tells of three young Hebrew captives, Shadrach, Meshach, and Abed-Nego, who refused to bow to a golden Babylonian idol. They were arrested and brought before King Nebuchadnezzar. He gave them a stark choice: bow to the image or be burned alive in a superheated furnace. They replied, "Our God will deliver us from your fiery furnace. But even if not, we will not serve your gods or worship your golden image" (Dan. 3:17–18, author's paraphrase). The three young men refused to compromise even in the face of death. Their integrity before God was dearer to them than their life on earth. Because of their faithfulness, God preserved them from harm when they were thrown into the fire.

The book of Hebrews tells of godly heroes who paid a price for their faithfulness. Some were mocked, scourged, and chained in prisons. Others were stoned, sawn in two, or slain by the sword. Some wandered in deserts and mountains—destitute, afflicted, tormented, and forced to clothe themselves in animal skins. Some of these heroes were vindicated in their lifetimes, but not all. Many were martyred for their faith. The writer tells us that God provided something better for them: the heavenly reward He promises to all who remain faithful in spite of the obstacles set before them.

When Helen Keller was only nineteen months old, she contracted a fever that left her deaf and blind. With the help of her beloved teacher, Anne Sullivan, Helen learned to read and write, becoming the first deaf-blind person to effectively communicate with the sighted and hearing world. This made her world-famous at the age of eight. Helen went on to attend high school and graduated from Radcliffe College.

At that point, already beloved and respected by the world, she could have had an easy, quiet life. Instead, she made a commitment: to help the deaf and blind in every way she could.

And she did. She appeared before state and national legislatures and international forums. She visited thirty-nine countries on five continents. She published fourteen books and numerous articles. She spoke about the needs and issues affecting the deaf and blind. She won numerous awards, met every president from Coolidge to Kennedy, and was called by Winston Churchill "the greatest woman of our age."

Think of the odds she faced in achieving her goals! For many of us who have sight and hearing, it would have been enough to graduate from college, more than enough to travel the world, beyond imagination to meet presidents. And yet, against insurmountable odds, Helen Keller kept her commitment. Known as a woman of integrity, she faced down the barricades and improved life for the deaf and blind the world over.[19]

It takes strength to live a life of integrity. As my friend Pat Williams wrote:

> People of integrity don't abandon their values and principles under pressure. They know that times of adversity and temptation are precisely when values and principles matter most. They keep promises. They fulfill obligations. They maintain their honor even when it is costly to do so.[20]

BE ACCOUNTABLE TO SOMEONE

"Love one another." "Instruct one another." "Be patient with one another." "Encourage one another." "Confess your sins to one another." There are more than forty "one another" passages in the

New Testament, telling us there's no such thing as a lone-ranger Christian. We are in relationship with one another, and we are accountable both to give and receive instruction to and from each other in the body of Christ.

The author of the book of Hebrews wrote: "Let us consider one another in order to stir up love and good works . . . exhorting one another" (Heb. 10:24–25).

Here the writer says that we should "stir" each other up to "love and good works." "To stir" means "to arouse, provoke, irritate, or exasperate."

Sometimes, integrity needs to be "provoked" or "aroused" in us by those around us. In *Christianity Today* Bill Hybels told this story about himself:

> One evening I stopped by the church just to encourage those who were there rehearsing for the spring musical. I didn't intend to stay long, so I parked my car next to the entrance. After a few minutes, I ran back to my car and drove home.
>
> The next morning I found a note in my office mailbox. It read: "A small thing, but Tuesday night when you came to rehearsal, you parked in the 'No Parking' area. A reaction from one of my crew (who did not recognize you until after you got out of the car) was, 'There's another jerk parking in the "No Parking" area!' We try hard not to allow people—even workers—to park anywhere other than the parking lots. I would appreciate your cooperation too." It was signed by a member of our maintenance staff.
>
> I'm sorry to report this staff member is no longer with us. He was late coming back for lunch the next day, and we had to let him go. You have to draw the line somewhere . . .

No, I'm kidding. Actually, he's still very much with us, and his stock went up in my book because he had the courage to write me about what could have been a slippage in my character. And he was right on the mark. As I drove up that night, I had thought, I shouldn't park here, but after all, I am the pastor. That translates: I'm an exception to the rules. But that employee wouldn't allow me to sneak down the road labeled "I'm an exception."

I'm not the exception to church rules, nor am I the exception to sexual rules or financial rules or any of God's rules. As a leader, I am not an exception; I'm to be the example. According to Scripture, I am to live in such a way that I can say, "Follow me. Park where I park. Live as I live."

That's why we all need people like my staff member to hold us accountable in even the small matters. Because when we keep the minor matters in line, we don't stumble over the larger ones.

Just when I was starting to think, I'm an exception, somebody on our staff cared enough to say, "Don't do it, Bill, not even in one small area." That's love.[21]

THE GREATEST COMPLIMENT

Several years ago I read a tale about a group of salesmen who were leaving a Chicago convention and were late getting to O'Hare Airport for their flight home. As they hurried into the terminal, they heard the last call for their flight. They began to run through the busy airport, dodging and weaving through the crowd, their carry-on luggage careening behind them. Two of the men crashed into a table stacked with beautiful gift baskets of apples, overturning it. Apples bounced and rolled everywhere, but the men kept running. They reached their gate just as it was closing and managed to board the plane.

All except one man. He stopped and told his companions to go on; he'd catch a later flight. Conscience-stricken, he turned back and found the young boy who managed the apple stand on his knees, in tears, groping for the scattered apples and baskets.

The salesman got on his knees beside the boy, gathered apples and baskets, and helped him set up the display again. Some of the baskets were damaged, many apples were bruised, and a few were missing. He opened his wallet and placed three large bills in the boy's hand. "Here. Take this," he said. "It will more than cover the cost of the damage. I'm very sorry we messed up your day. Are you okay, now?"

The boy nodded his thanks through his tears, and the salesman turned back to the lobby to arrange for a new flight home. He hadn't walked far before the boy called out, "Mister . . ." As he paused and turned around, the boy said, "Are you Jesus?"[22]

No one could receive a greater compliment than to be mistaken for Jesus. It happened to this man because he allowed himself "to be conformed to the image of His Son" (Rom. 8:29). That is the call laid on every Christian, and when we respond to it, we become faithful to the will of God and reflect His character. That is what it means to be a person of integrity.

The godly walk with integrity; blessed
are their children who follow them.

—PROVERBS 20:7 NLT

CHAPTER 8

A LIFE OF HUMILITY

Pride is always hungry and must
always be fed. Humility sustains itself.

In Detroit in the 1930s, three young men boarded a bus and attempted to pick a fight with a passenger sitting alone in the back. They threw one insult after another, but the man said nothing in response. Eventually the bus came to the man's stop. He stood, pulled a business card from his pocket, and handed it to one of the men before stepping off the bus and going on his way. It read: Joe Louis. Boxer.

The three young men had tried to pick a fight with the future heavyweight boxing champion of the world, a title Joe Louis held from 1937 to 1949. He could easily have given those men the fight they wanted, and no one would have blamed him. Yet he restrained himself, and the three lucky men were given a firsthand look at humility—power under control.[1]

That day on the bus, Joe Louis demonstrated a virtue that's commonly misunderstood and rarely pursued. In fact, humility is so misunderstood that it's often confused with traits that are negative or with weaknesses that are crippling. So let's take a moment to clear up the two most common mistakes about this remarkable virtue.

First, don't confuse humility with a lack of confidence or self-worth; those are not humility but low self-esteem.

According to Pat Williams, senior vice president of the pro basketball team the Orlando Magic, "a humiliated person feels weak and enslaved; a humble person feels strong to serve others. A humiliated person feels helpless and hopeless; a humble person feels helpful and hopeful. A humiliated person feels powerless and dishonored; a humble person feels empowered and dignified. Humiliation tears down; humility builds up. Humiliation is a tragedy; humility is a choice."[2]

A second common mistake is to equate humility with excessive self-deprecation. You know this person—the one who always manages to remind you how humble he is, who painstakingly points out how he sacrifices for others, who purposefully puts himself down to manipulate you into complimenting him. That's not humility; that's a martyr complex.

No one is born humble. Becoming humble takes effort, effort that is rewarded beyond measure. That's why the Bible tells us to seek humility:

- "Humble yourselves in the sight of the Lord, and He will lift you up" (James 4:10).
- "Therefore humble yourselves under the mighty hand of God, that He may exalt you in due time" (1 Peter 5:6).

And if we are told to seek it, then we can find it and learn it. Take comfort in this because humility is truly a challenging virtue. With that in mind, the next step toward humility is to understand what it is we seek.

WHAT IS HUMILITY?

Perhaps my favorite definition of humility is this: humility is the ability to use the power and resources we possess for the good of others.

The humble person values others, seeing value in them even when they themselves may not. He sees opportunities to serve others and does so naturally and easily, for the love of God, service, and those who benefit from his actions. He may be very successful in his work, but he still sees himself as a servant of all.

Humble people set and achieve personal goals, and they expect appropriate respect and appreciation for their work. They are not doormats. But they don't crave recognition, and their goal is not to be recognized above others.

A life of humility begins in the mind; it starts with how you perceive yourself. That means it's a decision you make, a mind-set you choose. Humility is not thinking less about yourself; it's thinking about yourself less. It's as simple (and challenging) as making life less about "me" and more about others.

In our day of selfies, self-promotion, and building carefully crafted personae on social media, true humility is a rare quality. But let me be clear: it always has been.

Throughout history, pride has often been the "virtue" of the day. Meanwhile, throughout the Bible and the writings of wise men and women of other faiths, pride is understood to be a vice. In fact, pride is the primary vice that leads to all kinds of other vices.

Most people are familiar with the proverb "Pride goes before destruction, and a haughty spirit before a fall" (Prov. 16:18). One of my favorite professors in seminary was the legendary Howard Hendricks. One time he told me he carried a little book that held the names of former students who'd either defected from the faith or had fallen into sin. He sought to understand if there was any consistent trait among them that would explain their failure. I'll never forget what he said he'd finally realized, "All but one of them were proud and arrogant."

If pride is such a negative quality, why have we spent the past several decades transforming it from a vice into a virtue?

Muhammad Ali once joked, "At home I'm a nice guy but I don't want the world to know. Humble people, I've found, don't get very far."[3]

Maybe you've seen that in your own life or in the lives of friends or coworkers. If you don't point people toward your successes, you might get passed over for promotions, or people won't appreciate you the way they should. Anyway, what's wrong with having a little pride in your own work and accomplishments? What's wrong with being recognized and praised?

Nothing. There is nothing wrong with being recognized for our accomplishments. It's when the recognition becomes our motive that we are in jeopardy. When we can feel joy in a job well done *only* if we're noticed and commended for it, then we're not doing our best work for the sake of the work; we're doing it for the sake of the praise we expect to get. We're not trying to benefit others with our work; we're trying to benefit ourselves. We're not glorifying God with our lives; we're stroking our own egos.

That kind of self-focus steals glory from God and steals away our own joy. When we begin to need praise and attention for everything we do, our happiness is completely dependent on other people noticing and flattering us. And when that doesn't happen, we feel deflated, worthless, bitter, even angry.

In contrast, a humble person doesn't depend on whether others notice her efforts. Her happiness isn't bound to what others think of her. Humility eliminates the anxiety that comes with the constant need to strive for greater recognition, position, and power. It takes the focus off of us and puts it back where it belongs—on God and on others.

Take note: The anxiety that accompanies pride is very real. Since pride always requires more—more recognition, more position, more power—we can never be at peace with our lives, and there's little room, energy, or genuine desire to lift up others. The anxiety that accompanies pride is spiritually exhausting.

But humility lifts all that off of us. We use our God-given talents to serve, to meet responsibilities, to enjoy what matters, to challenge ourselves to grow. We see value in others and rejoice in strengthening them for good purpose. We are spiritually fed by keeping our eyes and hearts on God and others.

In short, pride is always hungry and must always be fed.

Humility sustains itself.

THE GREATEST EXAMPLE

The greatest example of humility in all of history is the Lord Jesus Christ.

"The first image we have of Jesus is of him being born in a barn, surrounded by livestock. The scene announces humility, lowliness, vulnerability, weakness, exposure. The last image we get of Jesus as he ends his earthly life is as a broken body hanging on a cross. The scene communicates humiliation, suffering, failure and, to many, defeat. Neither the opening nor the closing scenes of Jesus' life suggest anything but a life of humble service."[4] And when Jesus said, "I am meek and lowly in heart" (Matt. 11:29 KJV), He gave us the secret to His life.

There are only two places in Scripture where it is explicitly stated that our Lord left us an example to follow, and one of them was an example of unparalleled humility.

On the day before He would be crucified, Jesus and His disciples gathered in a house to celebrate the Passover meal. As they finished the meal, the disciples began to argue among themselves as to which of them was the greatest. After spending three years with the greatest model of humility, they were bragging and comparing egos!

While His followers continued their dispute, Jesus rose from the table and crossed the room to a basin of water. Without a word, He took off His outer garment. Taking a towel, He wrapped it around His waist and tied it in the back. The disciples knew what this meant. They'd seen this many times before as the household slave washed their dusty feet when they entered a residence.

Then Jesus poured water into a basin and moved toward the disciple nearest Him. We can imagine a stunned silence falling over the disciples. In that atmosphere of bewilderment, Jesus kneeled and began to wash that disciple's feet. As He moved from man to man, the gleaming white towel turned brown. Two of the people whose feet Jesus washed that day were Peter, who would deny Him three times, and Judas, who would betray Him, both within mere hours.[5]

The purity of this act of humility is heightened by the fact that Jesus performed it while vividly conscious of His divine origin and nature. He knew He had come from God's presence and was about to return to God's presence. And yet, knowing this, He rose up and performed the lowliest of tasks.

This is the Son of the Highest stooping to the very lowest.

When He finished with this lowly task, Jesus said to His disciples, "Do you know what I have done to you? You call Me Teacher and Lord, and you say well, for so I am. If I then, your Lord and Teacher, have washed your feet, you also ought to wash one another's feet. For I have given you an example, that you should do as I have done to you" (John 13:12–15).

If we're looking for an unparalleled example of humility, we just found it.

When we read the accounts of our Lord's humility, it can seem as if humility is beyond our reach. But this quality of a life beyond amazing is available to you if you will follow the steps laid out for you in the Bible.

OWN YOUR PRIDE

Of all the sins against which the Bible continually warns, pride is one of the hardest for us to own. We can easily see it in others even when we can't see it in ourselves.

Several years ago, I jotted down a quip about a man who wrote a book with this title: *The Ten Most Humble Men in the World and How I Picked the Other Nine.*

The pastor of Moody Church in Chicago from 1929 to 1948, H. A. Ironside felt that he was not as humble as he thought he ought to be. And he asked an elder friend what he could do about it. His friend replied, "Make a sandwich board with the plan of salvation in Scripture on it and walk through the business and shopping area of downtown Chicago for a whole day."

Ironside followed his friend's advice. Upon completion of this humiliating experience, he returned home. As he took off the sandwich board, he caught himself thinking, *There's not another person in Chicago that would be willing to do a thing like that.*[6]

Here's the problem. As soon as we think we've finally become humble, if indeed we have, simply by recognizing that we have done so, we are prideful. We can avoid this trap by remembering that humility is a journey, a journey of devotion. It's not something you achieve; it's something you aspire to, something you embrace as a goal.

In his book *Life-Changing Love*, John Ortberg told this story:

Not long ago, there was a CEO of a Fortune 500 company who pulled into a service station to get gas. He went inside to pay, and when he came out he noticed his wife engaged in a deep discussion with the service station attendant. It turned out that she knew him. In fact, back in high school before she met her eventual husband, she used to date this man.

The CEO got in the car, and the two drove in silence. He was feeling pretty good about himself when he finally spoke: "I bet I know what you were thinking. I bet you were thinking you're glad you married me, a Fortune 500 CEO, and not him, a service station attendant."

"No, I was thinking if I'd married him, *he'd* be a Fortune 500 CEO and *you'd* be a service station attendant."[7]

Ouch! That stings, but being honest with ourselves about our own importance is a vital first step. The path to the amazing life of humility begins in the mind. It starts when we can honestly admit we have a problem with pride.

The apostle Paul wrote: "For I say, through the grace given to me, to everyone who is among you, not to think of himself more highly than he ought to think" (Rom. 12:3).

He went on to expose how the Christians in Rome valued some gifts and blessings of God above others and filled up with pride as a result of achieving those gifts. And indeed, it's when things are going well and we're experiencing successes and blessings that we're tempted to drift from humility into pride, as though we were the source of those blessings. It's during these times that we need others to help keep us grounded, as the CEO's wife did for him.

In our own lives, how can we take a similar step? Who in your family or your circle of friends can you trust to keep you grounded when you're tempted toward pride?

START SERVING

The single most powerful way to grow in humility is to start quietly serving. The concept of serving is found more than three hundred times in the Bible. Jesus said, "I am among you as the One who serves" (Luke 22:27).

When we start serving, we take our eyes off ourselves and begin to see things through the eyes of another.

Jesus said, "Whoever desires to become great among you, let him be your servant. And whoever desires to be first among you, let him be your slave. . . . But he who is greatest among you shall be your servant" (Matt. 20:26–27; 23:11).

From 1984 until 1986, Peggy Noonan was the White House speechwriter for President Ronald Reagan. In her book *When Character Was King*, she tells this story:

> A few days after President Reagan had been shot, when he was well enough to get out of bed, he wasn't feeling well, so he went into the bathroom that connected to his room. He slapped some water on his face and some of the water slopped out of the sink. He got some paper towels and got down on the floor to clean it up. An aide went in to check on him, and found the president of the United States on his hands and knees on the cold tile floor, mopping up water with paper towels. "Mr. President," the aide said, "what are you doing? Let the nurse clean that up!" And he said, "Oh, no. I made that mess, and I'd hate for the nurse to have to clean it up."[8]

Once you develop a realistic view of your own importance, you start to realize that every other person on earth is just as precious to God as you are—and just as deserving of love lived out in action.

This principle is expressed in Scripture. "Let nothing be done through selfish ambition or conceit, but in lowliness of mind let each esteem others better than himself. Let each of you look out not only for his own interests, but also for the interests of others" (Phil. 2:3–4).

William Barclay believed that serving others was one of the most practically helpful principles in the entire Bible:

> Every economic problem would be solved if men lived for what they could do for others and not for what they could get for

themselves. Every political problem would be solved if the ambition of men was only to serve others and not to enhance their own prestige. The divisions and disputes which tear the Church asunder would for the most part never occur if the only desire of the Church was to serve the Church, and not to care in what position as long as the service was given. When Jesus spoke of the supreme greatness and value of the man whose ambition was to be a servant He laid down one of the greatest practical truths in the world.[9]

KEEP LISTENING AND LEARNING

The Bible warns us repeatedly against being wise in our own eyes. Why is that so important? Because when we decide we are wise, we stop listening, we stop asking questions, we stop trying to learn. When we think we know it all, that's when arrogance and pride take over our lives.

Pablo Casals is considered one of the greatest cellists who ever lived. He played for Queen Victoria when he was twenty-two. He also played for President Kennedy when he was eighty-six! He was unquestionably a master of his instrument, yet at the age of ninety-six he still practiced at least three hours a day. When asked why, he said, "I'm beginning to notice some improvement."[10]

Casals achieved great and remarkable things, yet he never stopped learning, practicing, and trying to improve.

Pat Williams applied this important point to leadership when he wrote: "Humble leaders are always learning. They don't assume they have all the answers. They are humbly curious. They are always reading. They listen to the ideas of people around them, including subordinates. They encourage fresh insights from people at all levels, from board members to janitors."[11]

Katherine Graham, the longtime publisher of the *Washington Post,* was once asked what she considered to be the most important trait of the great leaders of the world whom she had met. She replied without hesitation, "The absence of arrogance."[12]

HANG OUT WITH ORDINARY PEOPLE

The apostle Paul wrote: "Do not set your mind on high things, but associate with the humble" (Rom. 12:16).

> Few kinds of pride are worse than snobbery. Snobs are obsessed with questions of status, with the stratification of society into "upper" and "lower" classes, or its division into distinctions of tribe and caste. . . . They forget that Jesus fraternized freely and naturally with social rejects, and calls his followers to do the same with equal freedom and naturalness.[13]

These are the words of John Stott—scholar, teacher, and pastor of the great All Souls Church in London. Stott had every earthly reason to be prideful. He was famous not only in the United Kingdom, where he lived, but all over the world. And yet Tim Chester, now a pastor, relates this story of his encounter with Stott at a conference in northeast England, where Stott was the featured speaker and Chester was just nineteen:

> When we arrived at the conference, the friend with whom I'd come went off and I was left alone, feeling out of place. An older man came over and began talking to me, asking me about myself.

After a few moments my friend returned and the man introduced himself, "Hello, I'm John Stott." My jaw nearly hit the floor. I'd been speaking to the great John Stott without realizing it. That moment made a big impression on me. John, who was the only speaker that day, had seen an awkward looking teenager on his own and took it upon himself to make him feel welcome. I met him a few times subsequently and he always remembered my name. The private John Stott was just as impressive as the public persona: gracious, humble, without affectation. I'm sure it was this humility that meant God could entrust him with the influence and success he received. It is hard to underestimate the impact he has had across the world.[14]

We live in a culture that idolizes people who make it big. We're not interested in ordinary. We want extraordinary! We don't want to be lowly. We want to be exalted!

Stott's words about snobbery and his example of humility should motivate us to ask ourselves some tough questions. Am I obsessed with, or made anxious by, my social status? Do I rank people by their wealth, possessions, influence, or job? Have I surrounded myself only with people I think can help me move up—in society, wealth, career, appearance?

STOP TAKING YOURSELF SO SERIOUSLY

It seems counterintuitive that humility should produce joy and pride should steal it, but it's undeniably the case. When you are humble, spending your mental energy on others rather than yourself, you find humor in things your former self would have found intolerable.

Most notably, you can laugh at yourself! Prideful people, consumed with their own importance, are constantly tending to their own images and personae. They cannot laugh at themselves.

Consider former president George W. Bush, who, like many presidents, endured years of ridicule at the hands of late-night comics. He was criticized for a lot of things, but especially for his unique ability to botch the English language. In March 2017, Bush appeared on *Jimmy Kimmel Live*. In the course of the interview, Kimmel asked him if the many unflattering impersonations of him upset him, and Bush replied they did not.

"No," Bush answered. "I love humor. and the best humor is when you make fun of yourself."[15]

When you let go of concern about what others think of you, you'll no longer experience the anxiety of trying to be as rich or smart or accomplished as the next person in the room. You'll be able to set aside that feeling of superiority when your skills or station in life make you stand out from the crowd. Instead of comparing yourself with others, you'll be able to enjoy them—and yourself.

Several years ago I was on a speaking assignment in the southern part of our country, and, as I often do, I decided to visit the local Christian bookstore. There seemed to be no one in the store, except a young girl who was standing behind the checkout desk. As I entered the store, I could tell that the young girl behind the counter was studying me. In a moment she came over to where I was standing and asked me, "Are you who I think you are?"

Before I could answer, she said excitedly, "Please don't leave. I'll be back in just a minute."

She disappeared into the back room, and when she came back, she was accompanied by another girl, who was carrying a stack of books.

They walked up to me, giggling, and handed me the books and asked, "Would you mind signing your books for us?" She then handed me six books written by Josh McDowell. I looked away so that she wouldn't see my smile. Then I signed "Josh McDowell" in the front of all six books, thanked them, and walked out of the store. In my heart, I heard a voice saying, "Jeremiah, you ain't no big deal."

SPEND TIME WITH CHILDREN

I believe children have been created by God to keep us humble.

I was invited in 2016 to participate in the prayer service held in the majestic National Cathedral in Washington, DC, after every presidential election. The newly elected president and his family are the honored guests, and they sit in the front row.

The event is televised internationally. All participants are required to attend a very elaborate rehearsal early in the morning, at which time a stern lecture is given about the importance of following the script to the last detail. Every word of every prayer and every scripture that is to be read is printed on the master script, and nothing is to be added or subtracted. There is to be no ad-libbing. None whatsoever!

The leader of the event then explained that the master copy of the program would be placed on the lectern, which was above the audience in a sort of surround-pulpit. Each participant was to turn the page so the next participant would have his script ready to read.

When it was my turn to read Romans 5:1–8, I mounted the stairs to the pulpit and panicked! There was no program book. The person who'd preceded me to the pulpit had taken the book with him when he finished reading his part.

I was now standing before the watching world, and—I know you'll find this hard to believe—I had not memorized Romans 5:1–8. I felt as if my whole life were passing before my eyes.

Fortunately, one of my friends who was to follow me to the pulpit had carried a copy of the New Testament with him and handed it to me. After what seemed like an eternity of fumbling through the thin pages of that Bible, I found Romans 5:1–8 and read it with as much authority as my trembling voice would allow.

When the event was over, my friend Johnnie Moore came up to me and said that my pause before the reading of the Scripture was very effective and brought a sense of great dignity and respect to the Scriptures. When I told him what actually happened, we were doubled over from laughing so hard!

But the most important response to that never-to-be-forgotten moment in my life came from my twelve-year-old granddaughter, Zandy. She'd watched all of this on television back in California. When I saw her after I came home, she offered this: "Poppy, for a preacher, it sure took you a long time to find Romans in your Bible." Children keep you laughing and humble all at the same time!

DON'T LOSE PERSPECTIVE

Long before Theodore Roosevelt became the twenty-sixth president of the United States, he was fascinated with God's creation. He loved the grandeur of the natural world. During his time in office, from 1901 to 1909, he established several national parks and national monuments to preserve what wild places were still left after decades of expansion of industry and agriculture across the continent.

It's said that one of Roosevelt's habits when he entertained guests at the White House was to take them to the back of the lawn when the day was over. He would gaze up into the sky and tell his guests to do the same. After looking up at the innumerable stars scattered across the vast black nothingness of space for a couple of minutes, he would say, "Gentlemen, I believe we are small enough now. Let's go to bed."

After a long day's work filled with tough decisions and stressful situations, Theodore Roosevelt, a big personality if there ever was one, looked up at the stars in order to put his own importance into perspective. The enormity of the universe made him feel small . . . small enough to sleep well at night. He was the leader of a great nation, a job that brought with it the burden of keeping millions of citizens under his charge safe and shepherding a store of natural resources few other countries possessed. Who could sleep with all that pressure? Indeed, we can see from presidential photos just how quickly the office ages those who take it on.

The Bible tells us of another man who led a great nation and felt the responsibility keenly. David wrote his thoughts in the book of the Bible we call the Psalms: "When I consider Your heavens, the work of Your fingers, the moon and the stars, which You have ordained, what is man that You are mindful of him, and the son of man that You visit him?" (Ps. 8:3–4).

Compared to the vastness and wonder of the skies, David was humbled and felt insignificant. But he didn't stop there. "For you have made him a little lower than the angels, and You have crowned him with glory and honor" (v. 5).

The psalmist made the connection between God's power and glory and the glory that's been given to man. The same God who keeps the planets in their orbits and tells the wind where to blow and causes the rain to fall and the sun to shine, has crowned you with glory and honor! You can trust that if He is powerful enough to create, sustain, and order the universe, He is powerful enough to sustain you. You do not have to make yourself bigger than you are. You do not carry the world on your shoulders. God carries it on His. And He still has room to carry you as well.

Humility is one of the most difficult virtues to cultivate in our time and place. But as with all qualities worth pursuing, God does not leave us to self-improvement of our own power. He gives us power through His Holy Spirit to grow more and more into the people He intends us to be. When we choose to humble ourselves, we place ourselves in the stream of God's grace. And this grace is what we all need to flourish in life. As you continually make decisions to humble yourself, expect God to hear your desires, guide you, lift you up, and revive your spirit!

> *He has shown you, O man, what is good;*
> *And what does the LORD require of you*
> *But to do justly,*
> *To love mercy,*
> *And to walk humbly with your God?*
>
> —MICAH 6:8

CHAPTER 9

A LIFE OF SELF-DISCIPLINE

When the wind is in your face, keep your
head down and pedal with all your strength.

In his bestselling book *Outliers: The Story of Success*, author Malcolm Gladwell explains how extraordinary people achieve their success. His examples include the Beatles, Bill Gates, star hockey players, successful pilots, and Silicon Valley billionaires. After studying how they reached the pinnacles of their professions, here's what Gladwell learned: Successful people practice. A lot. In fact, he believes there's a magic number of ten thousand hours of practice that moves you from the rank-and-file to outranking almost everyone else.

Think about it. Ten thousand hours of practice devoted to improving yourself. Sounds overwhelming, doesn't it? Who commits to such a thing?

You do! Remember, you're embarking on a journey to a new life. Each step of that journey brings blessings, personal growth, and spiritual rewards that will manifest in your life and in your heart. This practice isn't boring repetition; it's strategic. It's for you to live the fullness of life in Christ, for the glory of God.

Now think about doing that for one year, one month, and three weeks—which is what ten thousand hours is. Suddenly, ten thousand hours is nothing, because the journey you've embarked on is for the rest of your life.

In this chapter we consider the final gift God has given you to make that journey: self-discipline. I believe self-discipline is the "outlier" that explains why some Christians seem to soar and others barely get off the ground.

Remember Katie Ledecky's self-disciplined practice that made her an enduring world champion swimmer? Remember Pablo Casals's humble conviction that he could always improve through the self-discipline of daily practice—even in his nineties? Remember the relentless training and self-control that allowed Lt. Michael Murphy to show his love for his men by surviving until he completed a call for help?

Self-discipline is the secret ingredient to achieving a life beyond amazing. Each trait in this book requires your commitment to achieve it. That commitment is expressed through your stated prayerful desire for it, by asking the Holy Spirit to help you attain it, and then . . . (yes, you know by now what comes next) through your own actions.

Personal discipline—inspired, sustained, and encouraged by the greatest help of all, the indwelling Holy Spirit—is the motivation and force behind the right actions you take to produce the fruit of the Spirit and enjoy a life beyond amazing.

In Paul's description of the fruit of the Spirit, he lists "self-control" last. This placement is no mistake. "By occupying this final position, self-discipline assumes a place of strategic importance. . . . self-discipline is the summation of the previous eight qualities that the Spirit produces. The work of the Spirit reaches its consummation in self-control. This virtue enables us to realize every other aspect of spiritual fruit."[1]

Like all the other traits, this one isn't always easy. Yet from my experience as a pastor, as a fellow traveler on the same journey, and from my studies of those who journeyed this path before us, there are insights that help us understand how to build it into our lives.

But first, let's be clear about one important thing. In this chapter we talk about developing your self-discipline so you can achieve a life beyond amazing. The journey you take to reach that goal is yours, and it will be different from anyone else's. When you allow the Holy Spirit to guide your heart on this journey, the opportunities, choices, and priorities He presents are uniquely for you.

So don't fall into the trap of comparing yourself to others. Don't be discouraged if these traits don't seem to show up right away or don't seem as well expressed in your life as in someone else's. Instead, be kind to yourself, persevere, and lean on God when you need support.

WHAT IS SELF-DISCIPLINE?

Self-discipline is choosing to do what's right when you feel like doing what's wrong. It's knowing you can but deciding you won't. It's not eating all the popcorn before the movie starts.

My favorite description of this character trait is this: "The ability to maintain progress toward a goal even when you're not in the mood, don't feel like making the effort, would momentarily enjoy something else, or find working toward your goal downright unpleasant."[2]

The New Testament word used to describe this virtue is related to our English word *government*. In other words, self-discipline is about governing yourself. It's the ability to regulate your thoughts, emotions, and actions in a godly manner. It's postponing temporary, immediate gratification to achieve goals you know will bring lasting rewards and increased self-respect.

This character trait extends beyond your behavior or actions; it's also about your emotions and your thought life. In fact, the Bible tells us that it extends to every area of your life. When you are living a life of self-discipline, you will be able to do several things:

- Master your moods. "Whoever has no rule over his own spirit is like a city broken down, without walls" (Prov. 25:28).
- Tame your tongue. "He who guards his mouth preserves his life, but he who opens wide his lips shall have destruction" (Prov. 13:3).
- Regulate your reactions. "The discretion of a man makes him slow to anger, and his glory is to overlook a transgression" (Prov. 19:11).
- Control your calendar. "See then that you walk circumspectly, not as fools but as wise, redeeming the time, because the days are evil" (Eph. 5:15–16).
- Manage your money. "There is desirable treasure, and oil in the dwelling of the wise, but a foolish man squanders it" (Prov. 21:20).

- Bridle your body. "Each of you should know how to possess his own vessel in sanctification and honor" (1 Thess. 4:4).[3]

That is the description of a life worth living, a life that allows you to evidence all the other traits, knowing you have a strong foundation of strength and self-control! Like all the character traits we've discussed thus far, self-discipline is more than what we're expected to do—it's also something we receive:

> True self-control is a gift from above, produced in and through us by the Holy Spirit. Until we own that it is received from outside ourselves, rather than whipped up from within, the effort we give to control our own selves will redound to our praise, rather than God's.
>
> But we also need to note that self-control is not a gift we receive passively, but actively. We are not the source, but we are intimately involved. We open the gift and live it. Receiving the grace of self-control means taking it all the way in and then out into the actual exercise of the grace.[4]

WHY IS SELF-DISCIPLINE SO IMPORTANT?

Let's begin with the *why*. Peter reminds us that God has given us "all things that pertain to life and godliness" including the "exceedingly great and precious promises" (2 Peter 1:3–4).

After listing the remarkable spiritual assets God has bestowed on us, Peter doesn't say we can now coast our way through life. On the contrary, the very next verses read, "But also for this very reason, giving all diligence, add to your faith virtue, to virtue knowledge, to knowledge self-control, to self-control perseverance, to perseverance godliness, to godliness brotherly kindness, and to brotherly kindness love" (vv. 5–7).

What Peter was saying to his readers is this: "You've been given great resources; now go out and make every effort to realize the full potential of all that you are and have in Christ Jesus."

Jesus spoke of self-discipline and self-control with absolute clarity: Self-control is the first choice a person must make in order to be His disciple. He said that discipleship begins at the point of self-denial: "Whoever desires to come after Me, let him deny himself. . . . For whoever desires to save his life will lose it, but whoever loses his life for My sake and the gospel's will save it" (Mark 8:34–35).

Each day we make hundreds of choices about the direction of our lives. When what we *want* to do lines up with what we *should* do, these choices are simple. These are wonderful moments! But let's be honest; a lot of the time we simply don't feel like doing what we know is best for us or for others. And this is where self-discipline kicks in and carries us up the hill.

Christ wants us to overcome our own ambitions, unhealthy desires, pettiness, and schemes so we will reap the greater reward of living wholly for Him. From beginning to end, the Christian life is about learning to govern your mind, emotions, and actions according to God's Word.

THE TRUTH ABOUT SELF-DISCIPLINED PEOPLE

I believe we view this character trait all wrong. Our pleasure-seeking, celebrity-idolizing culture has ingrained in us that self-discipline is no fun, that it's boring drudgery, tedious, hard, and isolating. Of course we consider it with great trepidation!

But what if I told you this understanding is entirely wrong?

A recent article by Tara Schiller summed up the truth beautifully. I've adapted her article to share here with you because it explains how self-discipline isn't something you resign yourself to; it's a trait you can embrace with excitement!

Here's what self-disciplined people are really like:

1. **THEY'RE BETTER AT AVOIDING TEMPTATION AND ARE MORE SATISFIED WITH THEIR LIVES.** According to a recent study, self-disciplined people don't focus on deprivation; they focus on finding better ways to avoid temptation.[5] The perception is that self-discipline is pure self-denial that kills all the excitement and fun of life. But statistically, this isn't true. When you practice discipline, you're more confident about who you are, you learn to easily avoid pitfalls, and you get more of what you *really* want. This builds a deep satisfaction.

2. **THEY ENJOY CONQUERING THEMSELVES.** There's a thrill in conquering yourself. It builds your self-belief and gives you a lasting high, which further motivates you to continue challenging yourself. This is not a boring life without excitement, but rather a thrilling game of conquering your inner demons.

3. **THEY LIVE MORE FULLY IN THE MOMENT.** Working toward a bigger goal means you have to focus on choices you make in the moment. This requires you to be more aware of what's going on *right now*. So you experience life more fully, and you recognize how the people and environment you surround yourself with affect you. As a result, you put

yourself in more positive situations and remember them with more clarity.

4. **THEY'RE BETTER AT SETTING BOUNDARIES.** As you change to meet your goals, some people may work against you. Knowing this encourages you to set boundaries against those who stand in your way. For example, say you're trying to change eating habits. You may notice some people begin to sabotage your efforts; they'll buy you food presents, stock the freezer with your favorite ice cream, or invite you out for pizza and make you feel guilty for not socializing. Now that you see what's happening, you have the power to stop it.

5. **THEY ENJOY LIFE MORE AND DO MORE OF WHAT THEY WANT.** Self-discipline is born from a desire to move beyond a current situation and to break out of a comfort zone. To do this, you must decide what you *do* want out of life, and get rid of what you don't. Maybe you don't watch your favorite TV show because now you're absorbed in writing that book you always wanted to write!

   Self-discipline is viewed as constricting; but when you practice it, you see more clearly how your old culture, bad habits, and addictions were controlling you all along. Now you're freed from the guilt of doing things you knew weren't good for you. With your priorities covered, you can truly relax and have fun.

6. **THEY GET BETTER AT IT THE MORE THEY DO IT.** Self-discipline is a culture; the more you practice it, the more it becomes a part of your comfort zone. When you first started, you were fighting your old culture of immediate gratification. Now that old culture feels uncomfortable, and personal discipline gets easier and becomes what you desire.

7. **THEY'RE NOT PERFECT.** No one is disciplined all the time. Knowing this helps you to forgive yourself for relapses and continue moving forward toward your goals. This moving forward after failure is essential for success. As Ralph Waldo Emerson so eloquently put it, "Our greatest glory is not in never failing, but in rising up every time we fail."[6]

YOUR BATTLE FOR A DISCIPLINED LIFE

At the heart of self-discipline is the reality that each one of us has conflicting desires.

"What's your problem? Temper? Impatience? Self-control? Sex? Being honest? Your thought life? Pride? Laziness? Self-centeredness? Everyone has skeletons, and they don't always stay in the closet. You want to do right but you do wrong. . . . Sometimes you'd almost swear you were a split personality; a regular 'walking civil war.'"[7]

Every believer has two natures. He has an old nature with which he was born and a new nature, the nature of God, which he received when he was "born again," when he became a Christian. These two natures are in constant conflict, for the simple reason they are incompatible and irreconcilable. In his letter to the Galatians, Paul put it this way: "For the flesh [old nature] lusts against the Spirit [new nature], and the Spirit against the flesh; and these are contrary to one another, so that you do not do the things that you wish" (5:17).

In his letter to the Romans, Paul described the personal conflict that was raging in his own heart: "I don't really understand myself, for I want to do what is right, but I don't do it. Instead, I do what I hate. . . . I want to do what is good, but I don't. I don't want to do what is wrong, but I do it anyway" (Rom. 7:15, 19 NLT).

Years ago someone gave me a bit of poetic advice about these two natures that continues to instruct and encourage my life:

> *Two natures beat within my breast;*
> *The one is foul; the one is blest.*
> *The one I love; the one I hate.*
> *The one I feed will dominate.*

The Bible is relevant for every age, but its description of the battle for a disciplined life is especially significant for ours. Daniel Akst, author of the book *Temptation: Finding Self-Control in an Age of Excess*, described life in our modern Western culture as: "living at a giant all-you-can-eat buffet, one that offers more calories, credit, sex, intoxicants, and just about anything else we can take to excess. . . . With more possibilities for pleasure and fewer rules and constraints than ever before, the happy few will be those able to exercise self-control."[8]

More temptations, fewer rules. No wonder we can find this virtue so challenging to master.

THE BLESSINGS OF YOUR DISCIPLINED LIFE

The more we succeed in becoming self-disciplined, the more we grow in freedom, maturity, and peace of mind. Envision your life filled with a peace that passes understanding, a generosity that brings you the joy of Jesus Christ, a quiet endurance through difficulty, and a humility that provides lasting reassurance and perspective!

Harry S. Truman said, "In reading the lives of great men, I found that the first victory won was over themselves. Self-discipline with all of them came first."[9]

Anyone who ever set his or her mind to train or study for anything—whether a sport or a nursing career, a musical instrument or building a business, becoming an astronaut or saving to buy a house—knows that without self-control, our plans come to naught. We never get fit. The business fails before it has a chance to get off the ground. Buying the house has to be put off for another year. In the same way, when we lack self-control over our attitudes, actions, and words, we derail our relationships, our lives, and our spiritual growth.

"The purpose of self-control," says Maxie Dunnam, "is that we may be fit for God, fit for ourselves, and fit to be servants of others. . . . It is not a rigid, religious practice—discipline for discipline's sake. It is not dull drudgery aimed at exterminating laughter and joy. It is the doorway to true joy, true liberation from the stifling slavery of self-interest and fear."[10]

As we mature in life and faith, we increasingly experience the many benefits of self-discipline. Maturity in all things requires and depends on self-control. Think about what commonly derails all of us: impulsiveness, procrastination, giving in to unhealthy desires and habits, impatience, and anger. Without self-control, these impulses are our masters. When we have this trait, we master them.

In a May 2017 *Christianity Today* article titled "The Science of Sinning Less," sociologist Bradley Wright and psychiatrist David Carreon shared research showing that people with more self-control "live longer, are happier, get better grades, are less depressed, are more physically active, have lower resting heart rates, have less alcohol abuse, have more stable emotions, are more helpful to others, get better jobs, earn more money, have better marriages, are more faithful in marriage, and sleep better at night."[11]

Sounds pretty good! So let's take a new look at self-discipline, taking the fear and dread out of that word and replacing them with hope and excitement.

EMBRACE YOUR DISSATISFACTION

In a letter he wrote a few years before his death, Paul confessed to his friends in Philippi that he did not consider himself to have achieved his goal of following Christ (Phil. 3:12–14). He was at the zenith of his career, yet he realized that he had not reached the high-water mark of his calling. He had permeated major cities with the gospel, he had founded churches that continued to flourish, he had written major doctrinal letters that even today astound the scholars, but he was not satisfied with himself. The more he accomplished, the more he saw that needed to be accomplished.[12]

How could the greatest man who ever walked upon this earth, besides Jesus Christ, be at the end of his life and admit being dissatisfied with his spiritual progress?

But this was one of his spiritual secrets: Paul had an incurable hunger and thirst for God that drove him forward.

One of Jesus' beatitudes reads like this: "Blessed are those who hunger and thirst for righteousness, for they shall be filled" (Matt. 5:6). Take note: Jesus was pronouncing a blessing on "those who *hunger* and *thirst* for righteousness."

The first time I really understood those words was one of those times in my spiritual walk when I was discouraged with where I was. Then I discovered that hunger and thirst for more of God and more of His presence in my life was not a bad thing, but a very good thing. In fact, it is a blessed thing! God is honored when His children refuse to be complacent about their faith . . . when they hunger and thirst for more.

I truly believe the first step we take toward a life beyond amazing is realizing we're not satisfied with our present life. More than one motivational speaker that I have listened to over the years has expressed some version of this maxim: "Until the pain of staying the same becomes more acute than the pain of change, nothing happens. We simply maintain the status quo and we convince ourselves that playing it safe is safe."[13]

If we're not unhappy and dissatisfied with how much and what kind of love, joy, and peace we have in our lives, nothing will change. If we're not convicted that we fall short in generosity and compassion, we'll stay the same. And if we think we're humble and resilient when we're not, we fool ourselves and a life beyond amazing for us will just be a nice title to a new book.

So embrace your dissatisfaction with your life. Don't let it depress or discourage you. Remind yourself that the more you want a better life, the more power and fuel you have to achieve it!

BEWARE OF YOUR GOOD INTENTIONS

Reading a book like this can lull you into thinking you're responding when you're not. Looking back over my life, I remember times when I got a spiritual high from reading about the victories of others. This is called a vicarious blessing. But it's also a dangerous proposition. It can give you the feeling you're doing something when you're not. The time-worn statement that "the road to hell is paved with good intentions" perfectly summarizes what I'm trying to say.

While reading William Barclay's commentary on the gospel of Matthew, I came across this account of the life of the great poet Samuel Taylor Coleridge, author of one of the world's most famous poems, "The Rime of the Ancient Mariner."

> Coleridge is the supreme tragedy of indiscipline. Never did so great a mind produce so little. He left Cambridge University to join the army; he left the army because, in spite of all his erudition, he could not rub down a horse; he returned to Oxford and left without a degree. He began a paper called *The Watchman*, which lived for ten issues and then died. It has been said of him: "He lost himself in visions of work to be done, that always remained to be done. Coleridge had every poetic gift but one— the gift of sustained and concentrated effort." In his head and in his mind he had all kinds of books, as he said himself, "completed save for transcription. . . . I am on the eve of sending to the press two octavo volumes." But the books were never composed outside Coleridge's mind, because he would not face the discipline of sitting down to write them out. No one ever reached any eminence, and no one having reached it ever maintained it, without discipline.[14]

BEGIN WORKING OUT

When Paul wrote to young Timothy to instruct him in his Christian growth, he gave him the secret to godliness, which he'd learned through many years of study and practice: "Train yourself to be godly" (1 Tim. 4:7 NLT).

When Paul wrote to the Philippians, he told them: "Work out your own salvation" (Phil. 2:12).

"*Train* yourself" means train with a plan and with discipline. When the text says, "*work out* your own salvation," it means working something through to its full completion. Working out our salvation is working out what God has already worked in.

> Tom Landry, [legendary] coach of the Dallas Cowboys . . . said, "The job of a football coach is to make men do what they don't want to do in order to achieve what they've always wanted to be." In much the same way, Christians are called to make themselves do something they would not naturally do—pursue the Spiritual Disciplines—in order to become what they've always wanted to be, that is, like Jesus Christ.[15]

One way to master self-discipline is to create new habits. In his article "The Science of Sinning Less," Bradley Wright goes on to explain how he does that. There are three parts to a habit, he wrote. There's a behavior (what is done), a cue (when it is done), and a reward (why it is done). Put them together, practice regularly, and a habit emerges.

However, for big, challenging changes, Wright learned he had to take a different approach. Instead of starting a full exercise regimen all at once, he chose one small behavior, so small it felt trivial. This ensured it was easy to do. Then he did this small behavior consistently until it became routine. Then he added another small behavior from the big change until it, too, was routine. Then another, and another, until the whole big change became habit.

So every morning after he took his vitamins (the cue), he walked to a designated room and did one single exercise (the behavior).

That's it. One repetition of one exercise. When he finished, he told himself, out loud, "Good job!" (The reward). "My goal in doing one repetition was not to get good exercise. . . . My goal was building *the habit* of good exercise." Eventually, the full morning exercise routine became his habit, something he did "without a second thought."

Interestingly, other blessings began to show up. He was more disciplined in other areas of his life. (This is a typical side effect of increasing discipline in one area of your life—it gets easier to be disciplined in others!) Over several years, Wright formed new habits with exercise, eating, paying attention to his wife, helping his son with schoolwork, praying, being grateful, photographing nature, cleaning the house, meeting people at church, learning about his faith, and other things that matter to him.

"Intentional habit formation is central to the New Testament's call to holiness and sanctification," Wright said.[16]

TALK BACK TO YOUR BODY

In one of the great passages of the New Testament, the apostle Paul likens the Christian life to an Olympic event and zeroes in on the rigors of personal training involved in preparing for that event: "Don't you realize that in a race everyone runs, but only one person gets the prize? So run to win! All athletes are disciplined in their training. They do it to win a prize that will fade away, but we do it for an eternal prize" (1 Cor. 9:24–25 NLT).

Then Paul gives us his personal testimony. He applies the discipline of the Olympic competitor to his own personal walk with the Lord: "So I run with purpose in every step. I am not just shadowboxing. I discipline my body like an athlete, training it to do what it should. Otherwise, I fear that after preaching to others I myself might be disqualified" (vv. 26–27 NLT).

The older I get, the more this passage resonates with me. There are some days when my body tells me it doesn't want to obey me anymore. I actually have arguments with my body. I talk back to it!

My body wants to sleep; I need to get up! My body wants to eat; I've eaten enough! My body wants to stop exercising; if I stop I might not ever start again. My body resists the effort necessary to pray and read the Bible; I cannot let my body win this battle! My body wants to give up when the going gets tough; but I know I must go on!

This battle with our bodies is an all-inclusive struggle because "our bodies and our souls live so close together that they catch each other's diseases." I don't know who said this, but it has been in my spirit for more than thirty years. When I don't feel good physically, it has an impact on my spiritual life, and the opposite is also true.

I'm a beach bike bum. I love to ride my beach cruiser down the bike trail in Coronado. At certain times during the day there, the winds can be fierce. This was the case recently as I headed out to ride. On the way down to the beach, the wind was at my back, and I was flying so fast I could barely keep my feet on the pedals. At one point I stood up on my bike to rest my backside, and the wind was blowing so hard that without moving the pedals, my body became like a sail, and I flew along!

When I got to the end of my ride, I found my resting place, drank my water, and began preparing myself for a difficult ride home. Sure enough, I've never experienced anything like I did that day.

The wind was so fierce in my face that every stroke of the pedals was a challenge. I had to promise myself not to look ahead, or I'd never have had the courage to continue. Once, I decided to stand up again, and in that one moment my bike almost came to a dead stop! There was only one way to make it all the way home without repeatedly stopping: when the wind is in your face, keep your head down and pedal with all your strength.

Make this your mantra on the days when it feels as though the winds are fiercely blowing right at you. Don't think about how far you have to go. Don't think about quitting or resting. Keep your head down and keep pedaling! I made it home that day, and then I made a careful note of that ride and the time it occurred.

We all face difficult days. As I write this, it feels as if I've been riding against the wind in my life for the past few days, and it's not pleasant. I like the wind at my back. I prefer the easier ride, just like you do.

But I'm grateful for the experience on that trail and in life. I know I can keep moving forward if I keep my head down in submission to God and to His purposes, and if I go forward with all my heart and mind and strength. I must not yield to my puny human nature that wants me to quit pedaling. I will lean into the wind and keep moving forward. Sometimes it will be at a very slow pace, but I won't stop and I won't give up.

FAST-FORWARD YOUR LIFE

The writer of Hebrews captured this principle in the life of Jesus:

> We do this by keeping our eyes on Jesus, the champion who initiates and perfects our faith. Because of the joy awaiting him, he endured the cross, disregarding its shame. Now he is seated in the place of honor beside God's throne. Think of all the hostility

he endured from sinful people; then you won't become weary and give up. (Heb. 12:2–3 NLT)

This is the "greater yes" that enables us to say no to something lesser, the vision of a reality that can come to pass if we have the self-discipline to realize it.

I've never been much for awards shows on television, but a few years ago I ended up watching the Oscars and saw Matthew McConaughey accept the award for Best Actor. His acceptance speech was unlike anything I'd witnessed. Afterward, one of the announcers said he should have been given an additional Oscar for his acceptance speech.

He began his speech by saying there were only three things he needed every day: "something to look up to . . . something to look forward to, and . . . someone to chase."

He unashamedly acknowledged that he *looked up* to God, who "has graced my life with opportunities that I know are not of my hand or of any other human hand." He *looked forward* to his family: to his deceased father and to his mother, who was in the audience that night, to his two older brothers, and to his wife, Camila, and their three children.

But it was the *someone to chase* part of his speech I'll never forget:

When I was 15 years old, I had a very important person in my life come to me and say, "Who's your hero?" And I said, "I don't know, I gotta think about that. Give me a couple of weeks." I come back two weeks later, this person comes up and says, "Who's your hero?" I said, "I thought about it. You know who it is? It's me in 10 years." So I turned 25. Ten years later, that same person comes to me and says, "So, are you a hero?" And I was like, "Not even close. No, no, no." She said, "Why?" I said, "Because my hero's me at 35." So you see every day, every week, every month and every year of my life, my hero's always 10 years away. I'm never gonna be my hero. I'm not gonna attain that. I know I'm not, and that's just fine with me because that keeps me with somebody to keep on chasing.

So, to any of us, whatever those things are, whatever it is we look up to, whatever it is we look forward to, and whoever it is we're chasing, to that I say, "Amen." To that I say, "Alright, alright, alright."[17]

I was inspired by Matthew McConaughey's words. I want to keep getting better at following the Lord, loving my family, and growing as a person. When we have a vision for our future, self-discipline suddenly becomes much more attractive.

DISCOVER THE FREEDOM OF SELF-DISCIPLINE

"Self-discipline is a form of freedom," said H. A. Dorfman. "Freedom from laziness and lethargy, freedom from the expectations and demands of others, freedom from weakness and fear—and doubt."[18]

In 1981, when our family moved from Fort Wayne, Indiana, to San Diego, California, I took six weeks between assignments to travel with my family. I had a lot of time to think about how to reset my life and ministry. That was thirty-six years ago, and I want to report on one decision I made and how it affected my life.

For the first twelve years of my preaching, I'd gather together my notes, stories, and points; make a bullet-point outline; and then give the message. Toward the end of my time in Fort Wayne, I became concerned that I wasn't being as careful with my words as I should be, and that I'd developed some sloppy habits, including repeating the same phrases.

As I was about to enter this new phase of ministry, I felt prompted by the Holy Spirit to make a covenant: I would write out, word for word, every message I would preach from that point on for the rest of my life as a pastor.

The first couple of years, I wrote each message out longhand, and my secretary typed the manuscript. Eventually I became comfortable on the computer, and since then I have typed completely every message I've preached, with very few exceptions. That adds up to about 2,500 messages over thirty-six years.

Many blessings resulted from that covenant I made with myself and with God because of my discipline in carrying it out. I became more careful with my word choices, repetitions diminished, and a growing stockpile of notes and manuscripts on biblical messages accrued.

Then I started writing books based on these messages. Today the number of books totals more than seventy. Radio and television messages were presented with careful attribution of quotes and stories. Magazine articles and devotional material were harvested from these sermons. And in 2013, we released the *Jeremiah Study Bible*, which has more than eight thousand notes that came almost entirely from sermons preserved by writing them out before I preached them.

At first it was very difficult to make myself do this. But as time wore on, I began to enjoy this self-inflicted discipline. Today I can't imagine giving a sermon or major talk without first putting it in writing.

LIVE YOUR LIFE WITHOUT REGRET

Coronado is one of our family's favorite places to be. We love the beach on that island, one of the most beautiful in the world. Interestingly, Coronado is also home to the United States Navy's SEAL training camp. Sometimes I watch them or hear them, and I am always in awe of them. Recently a new book about the SEALs was released with the curious title *Make Your Bed*.

Written by Admiral William H. McRaven (US Navy Retired), the book is based on a commencement address he gave at the University of Texas at Austin in 2014. His speech went viral on the Internet, with millions of views. I watched the speech and read the transcript, and I hope this brief excerpt will motivate you to read the book as well. At the end of his book, Admiral McRaven talks about his experience as a SEAL:

> I stood at attention along with the other 150 students beginning the first day of SEAL training. The instructor, dressed in combat boots, khaki shorts, and a blue and gold tee shirt, walked across the large asphalt courtyard to a brass bell hanging in full view of all the trainees.
>
> "Gentlemen," he began. "Today is the first day of SEAL training. For the next six months you will undergo the toughest course of instruction in the United States military."
>
> I glanced around and could see some looks of apprehension on the faces of my fellow students.
>
> The instructor continued. "You will be tested like no time in your life." Pausing, he looked around the class of new "tadpoles." "Most of you will not make it through. I will see to that." He smiled. "I will do everything in my power to make you quit!"

He emphasized the last three words. "I will harass you unmerci-fully. I will embarrass you in front of your teammates. I will push you beyond your limits." Then a slight grin crossed his face. "And there will be pain. Lots and lots of pain."

Grabbing the bell, he pulled the rope hard and a loud clang-ing noise echoed across the courtyard. "But if you don't like the pain, if you don't like all the harassment, then there is an easy way out." He pulled the rope again and another wave of deep metallic sound reverberated off the buildings. "All you have to do to quit is ring this bell three times."

He let go of the rope tied to the bell's clapper. "Ring the bell and you won't have to get up early. Ring the bell and you won't have to do the long runs, the cold swims, or the obstacle course. Ring the bell and you can avoid all this pain."

Then the instructor glanced down at the asphalt and seemed to break from his prepared monologue. "But let me tell you something," he said. "If you quit, you will regret it for the rest of your life. Quitting never makes anything easier."

Six months later, there were only thirty-three of us standing at graduation. Some had taken the easy way out. They had quit, and my guess is the instructor was right, they would regret it for the rest of their lives.[19]

The journey to a life beyond amazing is a journey to the high-est, best, most love-filled life possible. It will not always be easy. But I promise you, it will be worth it. There will be times you'll fall down, or headwinds will force you to a stop. There will be times you doubt your worth and your strength, and any number of impediments will seem to block your progress.

Do not let this deter you in the greater journey. As you grow in self-discipline, you will grow in spiritual strength. That spiritual strength will reinforce your self-control; and I promise you, the more you pedal against the wind, the stronger you'll become.

Don't you realize that in a race everyone runs, but only
one person gets the prize? So run to win! All athletes are
disciplined in their training. They do it to win a prize
that will fade away, but we do it for an eternal prize.

—1 CORINTHIANS 9:24–25 NLT

CONCLUSION

It was 1979, and Donna and I were happily leading the Blackhawk Baptist Church in Fort Wayne, Indiana. This was my first church, our family was young, and I was learning every day how to serve a growing congregation. We'd completed two building projects, started a school, and had a weekend television program seen in five markets.

And that's when the defining decision in our shared life happened. A man by the name of Tim LaIIaye told me outright that I was going to be the next pastor of the church he had led for twenty-five years.

Over the next two years we resisted that message. How could God be in this? What did I know about ministering in California? But as we processed all of this, our lives were dominated by this opportunity.

Donna knew God was calling us to California, but I didn't want to see that. I was holding back, holding on to the church I'd started and was building. Finally, Donna said to me, "David, if God Himself were to come down here and tell you to go to California, I don't think it would change a thing!"

God didn't actually come down, but something pretty close

happened. One day we were discussing earthquakes—my latest excuse not to go. I reminded Donna that earthquakes were much more likely to occur in California than in Indiana. Sure enough, the very next day Fort Wayne, Indiana, had an earthquake. We discovered that God could send an earthquake wherever He chose, and we decided to go to California.

That one decision changed everything in our lives. It changed where our children went to school. It changed who they married. It changed where our twelve grandchildren would grow up. It changed what kind of ministry I would have. It opened doors that before were shut, and it shut doors that before were open.

THE FINAL DECISION

In the pages of this book, I've encouraged you to make nine decisions that will transform your life. But behind each of these decisions is one that impacts all of the others: What will you decide to do with the Lord Jesus Christ?

The Bible says Jesus came into this world to deliver us from a life of sin, selfishness, and separation from God. In our present state we "fall short of the glory of God" (Rom. 3:23). But through the death, burial, and resurrection of Jesus Christ, the barrier between our holy God and sinful man has been removed. When we decide to put our trust in Jesus Christ alone for eternal life and invite Him into our hearts and lives, He gives us the *life beyond amazing* you've been reading about in this book.

In the first nine chapters, we focused on what such a life might look like and how we might activate it in our everyday lives. Now you have one more decision to make: Will you embrace the Holy

Spirit, the person God gives to each of us to orchestrate this life beyond amazing?

THE POWER YOU NEED

On February 10, 2013, a fire broke out in an engine room of the Carnival cruise ship *Triumph* and knocked out the ship's power. The more than 4,200 passengers and crew were left in limbo, drifting in Gulf of Mexico currents. No power meant it was impossible to flush the toilets, keep cool under the blazing tropical sun, or preserve and cook all the perishable food on board. Passengers reported long lines for food, shortages of fresh water, illnesses, and widespread boredom. Many passengers slept in hallways or outside to escape the odors and heat below decks. The ship finally ported safely in Mobile, Alabama, four agonizing days later.[1]

The awful ordeal of the *Triumph* is a riveting reminder of what can happen when anything or anyone is disconnected from its source of power. For those of us who are Christians, our power source is the Holy Spirit.

You and I know there are millions who suffer darkness of spirit, who endure spiritual misery and pain, who have no hope and no relief. For them, the surge of power the Holy Spirit brings is instantly amazing. For others, it may feel like a more gradual process. But unless you embrace the power only the Holy Spirit can provide, you'll be running on empty.

If you've tried to sustain these nine character traits consistently in your life, you know how difficult it is. Maybe you've decided it's simply too difficult for you. You're right! It's not merely difficult to live the Christian life in your own power—it's impossible.

In the entire history of humanity, only one person has lived that kind of perfect life. That person is Jesus Christ. But even He did not live that life by His own power. Though He was one with God in heaven, to be a complete and perfect human, He had to live His life the way humans were created to live. He had to lay aside the independent use of His divine attributes; submit Himself to God the Father; and allow the Father's Spirit to live in Him, work through Him, and direct His life.

As Jesus told His disciples, "The words that I speak to you I do not speak on My own authority; but the Father who dwells in Me does the works" (John 14:10).

"Jesus lived, thought, worked, taught, conquered sin and won victories for God in the power of that same Spirit *whom we all may have*."[2]

The Spirit whom we all may have . . . if we accept Him.

EMBRACING THE HOLY SPIRIT

I hope that in reading this book you've developed a hunger for an amazing life. I pray that you long for a life empowered by the Holy Spirit, and that you're ready to hand over control of your life to Him. The natural question is, then, how do you do that?

There's a common misconception that when you become a Christian, the Holy Spirit suddenly surges into your life like an irresistible electrical current, and from that moment on you are totally Spirit-filled with no further action required on your part.

It's true that the Holy Spirit takes up residency in your life the moment you believe. But you do not, at that moment, instantaneously, become a fully matured believer. It takes time for His fruit to germinate and ripen. It requires careful tending of your spiritual soil.

It requires you to do your part, to submit to Him and then to do your work, the work He inspires you to do. Here are five specific steps that will lead you into a Spirit-empowered life.

Desire the Spirit

At the climax of one of Israel's festivals, Jesus stood up in the temple and said, "If anyone thirsts, let him come to Me and drink" (John 7:37). The next verse tells us that He was speaking of thirsting for the Holy Spirit. In another passage Jesus says our heavenly Father will "give the Holy Spirit to those who ask Him!" (Luke 11:13).

Both these passages indicate the same thing: We must desire the Holy Spirit to control us. We must thirst. We must ask for His direction.

Although the Holy Spirit wants to direct our lives, He doesn't override our free will or seize control of our minds. He works more like a combination of GPS and the power steering of your car. He gives you direction and then waits for your decision to follow Him. You have to decide to turn the wheel in the direction He points. Once you do that, He provides the power to steer the car and move it down the road. The direction to the destination and the power to get there belong to the Spirit, but the decision to continually drive forward to the correct destination remains with you.

So the first step is to want the Holy Spirit to guide your life and to be willing to follow Him when he does. You have to *want* a life beyond amazing; it won't happen unless you desire it above all else.

The late John Stott began each morning with this prayer, a confession of his desire for the Holy Spirit's help in his life:

Heavenly Father, I pray that this day I may live in your presence and please you more and more.

Lord Jesus, I pray that this day I may take up my cross and follow you.

Holy Spirit, I pray that this day you will fill me with yourself and cause your fruit to ripen in my life: love, joy, peace, patience, kindness, goodness, faithfulness, gentleness, and self-control.[3]

Renounce Your Sin

I love to remind people that the first name of the Holy Spirit is "Holy." Because He is holy, the Holy Spirit cannot thrive in a contaminated environment. The apostle Paul wrote: "Do not bring sorrow to God's Holy Spirit by the way you live. Remember, he has identified you as his own, guaranteeing that you will be saved on the day of redemption" (Eph. 4:30 NLT).

One of the classes that most impacted my life during seminary was a course taught by Dr. Charles Ryrie. It was on the Holy Spirit. In the years since, I have returned to Dr. Ryrie's book on the Holy Spirit time and again. In fact, it's one of the most marked-up books in my library. In that book he wrote:

> The victorious life or the life which does not grieve the Holy Spirit is the undefeated life. It is the life which is constantly responding to the light as it is revealed in God's Word. As response is made, this will bring to light more areas of darkness which then need to be confessed. Then more light comes, which in turn requires more confession of newly discovered darkness. And so it goes throughout life, but this is the normally developing life which grieves not the Spirit.[4]

When we confess our sins and determine to turn away from them (which is what the Bible calls repentance), the Lord forgives us. The apostle John wrote: "If we confess our sins, He is faithful and just to forgive us our sins and to cleanse us from all unrighteousness" (1 John 1:9).

By the power of Christ's atoning sacrifice on the cross, He willingly forgives those sins we confess and turn away from. By that forgiveness we are cleansed, and the Holy Spirit is set free to work in us and through us.

Devote Yourself to God's Word

As we discussed in the introduction, salvation is not an end. It's a beginning. It's the start of a lifelong process called sanctification, in which we participate with God, primarily through the study of His Word. We read the Bible to learn how to live the Christian life.

If you want the fruit of love to develop in your life, study the passages that show you what real love looks like, such as 1 Corinthians 13. If you want to learn how to endure, study the lives of men like Job or Moses. Do you want to grow in integrity? I suggest you get acquainted with Noah, Abraham, Joseph, Hannah, and Daniel.

Every day we face situations that require decisions. If we're to make the right decisions, to "be ready for every good work" (Titus 3:1), we must store up as much of His Word in our hearts as we can. That way, when those moments come, the Holy Spirit can bring to our minds the passage, principle, or concept from Scripture that will guide us.

I liken this to what happens when we use our computers. We store information on the hard drive, and then the operating system uses that information to accomplish the given task. Studying and memorizing the Word of God is like loading up your spiritual hard drive with great information. The Holy Spirit—your Operating System—uses what you've stored to operate your life.

But if you don't put anything on your spiritual hard drive, the Holy Spirit has nothing with which to work. This is a very simple but profound concept. Commit to spending time in the Scriptures every day, and over time you'll discover the fruit of the Spirit ripening in your life.

Let Go of Your Own Ambition

In the verses that immediately follow the listing of the fruit of the Spirit, Paul says, "And those who are Christ's have crucified the flesh with its passions and desires. If we live in the Spirit, let us also walk in the Spirit" (Gal. 5:24–25).

We are commanded to walk in the Spirit. It's simply a matter of obedience. We must be willing to let God be God in us. All God's resources will be available to us if we simply let the Holy Spirit take control of our lives.

Consider Paul's use of the word *walk*. It paints a simple but powerful picture of a person taking one step at a time. Sometimes they are very small steps, once in while they are big steps, sometimes they're steps into the wind, and other times they're steps with the wind. No matter—regardless of the pace, this person who is walking in the Spirit is continually making progress.

Letting go of our ambition may be the most difficult of the five steps, but it's also one of your most powerful catalysts to change. Paul tells us that if we want a Spirit-led life, we must be willing to abandon the path we've chosen for ourselves in favor of the one to which God calls us.

Jesus laid down this rule in His description of what it means to become His disciple. "If anyone desires to come after Me, let him deny himself, and take up his cross, and follow Me. For whoever desires to save his life will lose it, but whoever loses his life for My sake will find it" (Matt. 16:24–25).

It's a tough teaching in our ambitious age, but "no servant can serve two masters!" Your life has no room for two CEOs. Either you will be in charge, and you probably already know where that's headed, or you can place the Holy Spirit in charge. The Holy Spirit is the only one who can lead you into a life filled with the nine attributes we've been examining in this book.

Letting go of your ambition may seem risky, but you have the Bible's assurance that it's the only way to a life beyond amazing. And a tremendous reward will be waiting for you at the end when you hear Christ say, "Well done, good and faithful servant; you were faithful over a few things, I will make you ruler over many things. Enter into the joy of your lord" (Matt. 25:21).

Commit to the Spirit's Direction

Imagine yourself as a house. God comes in to rebuild that house. At first, you understand what He's doing. He's getting the drains right and fixing the leaks in the roof and so on. You knew those jobs needed doing, so you're not surprised. But presently He starts knocking the house about in a way that hurts and doesn't seem to make sense. What's He up to?

God is building a far different house from the one you imagined! You thought you were going to be made into a decent little cottage. But He's not content with a cottage. He's building a palace, an edifice worthy of Himself in which to live.[5]

So the question is, just what do you want your life to be like? A cottage or a palace? Do you desire the nine virtues of a good and joyful life enough to turn your life over to the Holy Spirit? Or do you want to retain control and risk the works of the flesh inching their way into more of your life and leading you further from all possibility of joy? This is not merely a onetime choice, but an ongoing decision Christians face throughout life. We must exercise constant vigilance over our lives and activities, constant openness to the expanded presence of the Holy Spirit, and constant repentance and recommitment each time we drift away from His direction.

The apostle Paul places this choice starkly before us: "For if you live according to the flesh you will die; but if by the Spirit you put to death the deeds of the body, you will live. For as many as are led by the Spirit of God, these are sons of God" (Rom. 8:13–14).

EVERYDAY TRANSFORMATION

Now that you know how to be empowered by the Holy Spirit, what comes next? What will your life be like when you're led by the Spirit of God? Will all potholes be filled? All detours straightened? All doors opened?

No, being Spirit-led doesn't mean your world suddenly becomes the garden of Eden. You'll still deal with the crabgrass and storm clouds of life, but you'll see a huge difference in how you deal with them.

With the Holy Spirit at home in your heart, the nine virtues will begin to grow. As you nourish them with God's Word and repair them with repentance, they will mature you into a person ready to face each day with confidence and joy. And along the way there will be blessings. You will *feel* the presence of the Holy Spirit in your life. You will enjoy a closeness in your walk with God that you never imagined.

The fruit of Spirit is about transformation—making you into something as different from what you were as a butterfly differs from a caterpillar; turning you from a creature that crawls into one that soars. It is by the immeasurable love and grace of God that He offers us His own power to do what we cannot do for ourselves.

Our initial attempts at walking under the control of the Holy Spirit are usually fumbling and ineffective, but He pays us the compliment of taking our attempts seriously and applauding them for the desire they display. In fact, He does even better than that. He not only hears what we intend; but, by the power of His Holy Spirit, He also turns our fumbling efforts into glorious masterpieces.

DON'T QUIT; KEEP PLAYING

There is a tale about a mother who had a young son who was struggling to learn how to play the piano. Thinking it might encourage him, she took him to a concert of a great pianist. After they were seated, the mother spotted a friend and left her seat to greet her. Her son, always curious, took the opportunity to explore the grand music hall. Soon he wandered through a door marked "Do Not Enter."

When the house lights dimmed, the mother returned to her seat and discovered her child was missing. Before she could react, the curtains opened on the spotlighted center stage, and the audience erupted with a mix of laughter and anger. When the mother saw the cause of their reaction, she gasped in horror. There at the keyboard sat her little boy, innocently picking out "Twinkle, Twinkle Little Star."

At that moment the master pianist made his entrance, quickly moving to the piano. He whispered in the boy's ear, "Don't quit; keep playing." He then leaned over the boy and with his left hand began filling in a bass accompaniment. A moment later his right arm reached around to the other side and added a running obbligato. When the last note sounded, the mesmerized audience thundered its applause. Together the old master and the young novice had transformed an awkward situation into a wonderfully creative experience.

This is what God does with us. No matter how hard we try to live godly lives, our efforts come up short. But when God enters, he turns our halting music into a masterpiece. This is what Paul was telling us when he wrote, "Work out your own salvation with fear and trembling; for it is God who works in you both to will and to do for His good pleasure" (Phil. 2:12–13). We provide the effort with our desire, our study, and our repentance. But it is God who provides the power by working in us to do His will. The result is a beautiful, transformed life.

The indispensable key, as the piano master told the little boy, is, "Don't quit; keep playing."

ACKNOWLEDGMENTS

First of all, I begin with an acknowledgment of how blessed I have been to be married to Donna for fifty-four years. When I first met her back in college, she was a cheerleader who led cheers for the basketball team on which I played. She has continued to be the number-one cheerleader in my life, and her love and support are the reasons I keep writing. I could not do it without you, Donna. You are truly "The Wife Beyond Amazing!"

While the two of us stand together in the middle of the circle, we are not alone. Our older son, David Michael, is in on everything we do. He leads the Turning Point media organization, including the rallies that feature our books. Diane Sutherland directs traffic, and some days it feels as if we are trying to negotiate one of those roundabouts or traffic circles that dominate the East Coast. Somehow she keeps us all going in the right direction and minimizes the traffic jams. What she does is incredible, and I am not the only one who notices!

The whole writing and editing team is headed up by Beau Sager. Over the last few years, as we have been privileged to work together, we have developed a close bond. It is true that he works for me, but it is even more true that we work together. We have developed a great partnership in the publishing of biblical materials.

Members of Beau's team include some great writers, researchers, and editors. Erin Bartels, William Kruidenier, Rob Morgan, and Tom Williams contributed to the final product that you hold in your hands. Thank you all for always being willing to join us as we pursue these important projects.

This year we added a new member to our team. Her name is Jennifer Hansen, and she has helped us to map out our chapters and has also been the final in-house editor on the book. It has been a great "first time" for us to work together, and I am certain it won't be the last.

Our creative team, led by Paul Joiner, has been way out in front on this book. Their marketing plan is also beyond amazing. It includes a one-hour, made-for-television interview with Sheila Walsh and what they are calling "The Amazing Conversation," featuring David Green, founder of the Hobby Lobby organization; Kirk Cousins, quarterback of the Washington Redskins; California pastor Bobby Schuller; and *American Idol* contestant and contemporary Christian singer Mandisa. That's right; we all are going to talk about "A Life Beyond Amazing." Sometime in the near future you will be a part of the discussion.

This is our second book with Thomas Nelson Publishers, and once again we have been privileged to work with Matt Baugher. It was Matt who originally suggested we do a different kind of book, and his ideas were among the first to help get this focused. Matt, our phone calls have meant much to me, and your suggestions have almost all been incorporated into the final product.

Sealy Yates has been my literary agent for more than twenty-five years. He also chairs the board of Turning Point ministries and is a very close, personal friend. And thank you also to Johnnie Moore, our ministry publicist and the national publicist for *A Life Beyond Amazing*.

Finally, all praise be to Jesus Christ! This "Life Beyond Amazing" is His life being poured into us by the Holy Spirit. In all of the world, there is nothing more amazing than that!

NOTES

Introduction

1. N. T. Wright, *After You Believe* (New York: HarperOne, 2011), 3, 7.
2. Bono, The Edge, Adam Clayton, and Larry Mullen Jr. with Neil McCormick, *U2 by U2* (New York: HarperCollins, 2006), 7.
3. Pat Goggins, "Character, the One Thing that Goes in the Casket with You," *Western Ag Reporter*, January 7, 2016, Buckaroo Guide's Facebook page, accessed July 27, 2017, https://www.facebook.com/buckarooguide/posts/1006454889413934

Chapter 1: A Life of Love

1. G. K. Chesterton, *Orthodoxy* (New York: Dodd, Mead & Company, 1959), 50.
2. Lewis B. Smedes, *Love Within Limits* (Grand Rapids: Eerdmans, 1978), 23.
3. Lewis B. Smedes, *Caring and Commitment* (San Francisco: Harper & Row Publishers, 1988), 26–27.
4. Quoted by Ray C. Stedman, "The One Commandment," Authentic Christianity, accessed May 30, 2017, https://www.raystedman.org/new-testament/john/the-one-commandment.
5. Philip D. Kenneson, *Life on the Vine* (Downers Grove, IL: InterVarsity, 1999), 42.
6. Quoted by Stedman, "The One Commandment."
7. Ray Ortlund, "'One Anothers' I Can't Find in the New Testament," *The Gospel Coalition* (blog), March 30, 2017, https://blogs.thegospelcoalition.org/rayortlund/2017/03/30/one-anothers-i-cant-find-in-the-new-testament-2/.

8. Barbara Starr and John Helton, "Medal of Honor Awarded to 'Antithesis of a Warrior,'" CNN, accessed May 30, 2017, http://www .cnn.com/2007/POLITICS/10/22/murphy.medal.of.honor/index .html?eref=yahoo#cnnSTCText.

9. Adapted from Ray C. Stedman, "That You Might Be Rich," *Authentic Christianity*, accessed May 30, 2017, https://www.raystedman.org /thematic-studies/christian-living/that-you-might-be-rich.

10. C. S. Lewis, *The Four Loves* (New York: HarperCollins, 1960), 155–56.

11. Lisa M. Fenn, "'Carry On': Why I Stayed," ESPN, August 15, 2016, http://www.espn.com/espn/otl/story/_/id/9454322/why-stayed.

12. Craig Brian Larson, *Illustrations for Preaching & Teaching* (Grand Rapids: Baker, 1993), 472.

Chapter 2: A Life of Joy

1. Gretchen Rubin, *The Happiness Project* (New York: Harper, 2009), 1–4.

2. Taken from Edward K. Rowell, ed., *1001 Quotes, Illustrations, and Humorous Stories for Preachers, Teachers, and Writers* (Grand Rapids: Baker Books, 2008), 177, 220.

3. Matt McMillen, "Richer Countries Have Higher Depression Rates," WebMD, July 26, 2011, http://www.webmd.com/depression/news /20110726/richer-countries-have-higher-depression-rates#1.

4. "Facts and Statistics," Anxiety and Depression Association of America, accessed June 5, 2017, https://www.adaa.org/about-adaa/press-room /facts-statistics.

5. Sabrina Tavernise, "U.S. Suicide Rate Surges to a 30-Year High," *New York Times*, April 22, 2016, https://www.nytimes.com/2016/04/22 /health/us-suicide-rate-surges-to-a-30-year-high.html.

6. McMillen, "Richer Countries Have Higher Depression Rates."

7. J. P. Moreland and Klaus Issler, *The Lost Virtue of Happiness* (Colorado Springs: NavPress, 2006), 14–15.

8. Jennifer Maggio, "Embracing Gratitude in Every Season," *iBelieve* (blog), February 22, 2017, http://www.ibelieve.com/blogs/jennifer-maggio /embracing-gratitude-in-every-season.html.

9. Philip Yancey, *Where Is God When It Hurts?* (Grand Rapids: Zondervan, 1990), Kindle locations 1697–1702.

10. Tony Snow, "Cancer's Unexpected Blessings," *Christianity Today*, July 20, 2007, http://www.christianitytoday.com/ct/2007/july/25.30.html.

11. G. K. Chesterton, *Orthodoxy* (New York: John Lane, 1909), 298.

12. Bruce Larson, *There's a Lot More to Health than Not Being Sick*, as quoted in Charles R. Swindoll, *Swindoll's Ultimate Book of Illustrations and Quotes* (Nashville: Thomas Nelson, 1998), 322.

13. Taken from Philip Kenneson, *Life on the Vine* (Downers Grove, IL: InterVarsity, 1999), 61.

14. Lewis B. Smedes, *How Can It Be All Right When Everything Is All Wrong?* (Colorado Springs: WaterBrook, 1999), 27.

15. Robert J. Morgan, *100 Bible Verses Everyone Should Know by Heart* (Nashville: B&H, 2010), Kindle locations 1833–34.

16. C. S. Lewis, *Mere Christianity* (New York: HarperCollins, 1980), 84.

17. Tony Reinke, "A (Very) Short Prayer for Joy Seekers," *Desiring God*, January 9, 2013, http://www.desiringgod.org/articles/a-very-short-prayer-for-joy-seekers.

18. Joni Eareckson Tada, "Joy Hard Won," Preaching Today, accessed June 5, 2017, http://www.preachingtoday.com/illustrations/2000/november/12692.html.

19. William Barclay, *Growing in Christian Faith* (Louisville: Westminster John Knox, 2000), 13.

20. Billy Graham, *Just as I Am* (San Francisco: HarperSanFrancisco, 1997), 697.

Chapter 3: A Life of Peace

1. Sarah Lebhar Hall, "A 3,000 Year Old Version of 'Imagine,'" *Christianity Today*, December 22, 2015, http://www.christianitytoday.com/ct/2015/december-web-only/3000-year-old-version-of-imagine.html.

2. Dr. David Jeremiah, "The Fruit of the Spirit Is Peace," September 26, 1982, Shadow Mountain Community Church.

3. Darryl Dash, "Prince of Peace," *DashHouse*, December 26, 2004, https://dashhouse.com/?s=prince+of+peace.

4. Ray Stedman, *Spiritual Warfare* (Waco, TX: Word Books, 1995), 77.

5. *Mundane Faithfulness* (blog), accessed July 14, 2017, http://www.mundanefaithfulness.com/about/.

6. "Homecoming," *Mundane Faithfulness* (blog), accessed July 14, 2017, http://www.mundanefaithfulness.com/home/2015/3/22/homecoming.

7. Author's paraphrase of Stedman, *Spiritual Warfare*, 77–78.

8. Sinclair B. Ferguson, *Deserted by God?* (Edinburgh: Banner of Truth, 1993), 51.

9. Henri J. M. Nouwen, *The Path of Peace* (New York: Crossroad, 1995), 78.

10. David J. Fant, *The Bible in New York* (New York: New York Bible Society, 1948), 66–67.

11. Norman B. Harrison, *His Peace* (Minneapolis: Harrison Service, 1943), 14.

Chapter 4: A Life of Endurance

1. Leo Tolstoy, *War and Peace* (UK: Penguin Books, 2005), Kindle location 23463.

2. Dr. Rachel Bryant, "Children Learn When They Persevere," *Star-Gazette*, January 11, 2006.

3. Dave Sheinin, "How Katie Ledecky Became Better at Swimming than Anyone Is at Anything," *Washington Post*, June 24, 2016, https://www .washingtonpost.com/sports/olympics/how-katie-ledecky-became -better-at-swimming-than-anyone-is-at-anything/2016/06/23/01933534 -2f31-11e6-9b37-42985f6a265c_story.html?utm_term=.3e87345250cb.

4. Kavitha A. Davison, "Why We Should Frame Katie Ledecky's Dominance in Terms of Women's Sports—Not Men's," *Voices* (espnW blog), August 9, 2016, http://www.espn.com/espnw/voices/article /17251015/why-frame-katie-ledecky-dominance-terms-women-sports -not-mens, video at 1:30:00.

5. Robert St. John, *The Life Story of Ben Yehuda* (Noble, OK: Balfour, 2013), Kindle locations 195–98.

6. Ibid., Kindle locations 80–81.

7. Ibid., Kindle locations 6411–13.

8. Ibid., Kindle locations 6411–22.

9. Harriet Beecher Stowe, *Oldtown Folks* (Boston and New York: Houghton Mifflin, 1911), 132.

10. From the publisher's description of Angela Duckworth, *Grit: The Power of Passion and Perseverance*, Simon and Schuster, accessed May 25, 2017, http://www.simonandschuster.com/books/Grit/Angela-Duckworth /9781501111105.

11. Angela Duckworth, *Grit: The Power of Passion and Perseverance* (New York: Scribner, 2016), 275.

12. Ibid., 46.

13. Irving Stone, quoted in Pat Williams and Jim Denney, *Go for the Magic!* (Nashville: Thomas Nelson, 1995), 175–76.

14. Erik Weihenmayer, *Touch the Top of the World* (New York: Plume, 2002).

15. John Phillips, *Exploring Hebrews* (Grand Rapids: Kregel, 1988), 177.

16. Jim Collins, *Good to Great* (New York: HarperCollins, 2001), 206.

Chapter 5: A Life of Compassion

1. Allie Torgan, "Grandparents Step Up, Save Families," CNN, July 25, 2013, http://www.cnn.com/2013/07/25/living/cnnheroes-de-toledo -grandparents/index.html.

2. Charles R. Swindoll, *Compassion* (Waco, TX: Word Books, 1984), 28–29.

3. Adapted from David Jeremiah, *Signs of Life* (Nashville: Thomas Nelson, 2007), ix.

4. Adapted from David Jeremiah, *Living with Confidence in a Chaotic World* (Nashville: Thomas Nelson, 2009), 39.

5. Jeremiah, *Signs of Life*, 216.

6. Original source unknown.

7. Andrew Arroyo, personal correspondence to author, dated May 27, 2017.

8. Alice Gray, *Stories for the Heart: The Second Collection* (Colorado Springs: Multnomah, 2001), 40–41.

Chapter 6: A Life of Generosity

1. Jim Dwyer, "Philanthropist Wants to Be Rid of His Last $1.5 Billion," *New York Times*, August 7, 2012, http://www.nytimes.com/2012/08/08 /nyregion/a-billionaire-philanthropist-struggles-to-go-broke.html.

2. Madeline Stone, "It Was Bill Gates' Mother Who Pushed Him into Philanthropy After He Became a Billionaire," *Business Insider*, May 10, 2015, http://www.businessinsider.com/bill-gates-mother-inspired -philanthropy-2015-5.

3. Bill and Melinda Gates Foundation, "Who We Are: Foundation Fact Sheet," accessed May 25, 2017, http://www.gatesfoundation.org/Who -We-Are/General-Information/Foundation-Factsheet.

4. Eleanor Goldberg, "Legendary Shoe Shiner Who Donated All His Tips ($220,000!) Retires . . . but Not from Our Hearts," *Huffington Post*, December 19, 2013, http://www.huffingtonpost.com/2013/12/19 /albert-lexie-shoe-shiner_n_4474990.html.

5. "Generosity of Spirit," Baylor University website, accessed May 25, 2017, http://www.baylor.edu/content/services/document.php/253576.pdf.

6. See entry for *ptōchos* at Blue Letter Bible, accessed May 25, 2017, https://www.blueletterbible.org/lang/lexicon/lexicon.cfm?Strongs=G4434&t=KJV.

7. Kelly M. Kapic and Justin L. Borger, *God So Loved, He Gave: Entering the Movement of Divine Generosity* (Grand Rapids: Zondervan, 2010), 147–48.

8. Michael Card, *Mark: The Gospel of Passion* (Downers Grove, IL: InterVarsity, 2012), 155.

9. G. Campbell Morgan, *The Gospel According to Mark* (Westwood, NJ: Revell, 1927), 271.

10. James A. Brooks, *The New American Commentary: Mark* (Nashville: Broadman Press, 1991), 203.

11. R. Kent Hughes, *Mark*, vol. 2 (Wheaton, IL: Crossway, 1989), 132–33.

12. Arno C. Gaebelein, *The Gospel of Matthew* (New York: Loizeaux Brothers, 1961), 555.

13. Douglas V. Henry, "Generosity of Spirit," Baylor University, Institute for Faith and Learning, 2015, accessed May 26, 2017, http://www.baylor.edu/content/services/document.php/253573.pdf.

14. Christian Smith and Hilary Davidson, *The Paradox of Generosity* (Oxford: Oxford University Press, 2014), 102.

15. Mike Holmes, "What Would Happen If the Church Tithed?" *Relevant*, March 8, 2016, https://relevantmagazine.com/god/church/what-would-happen-if-church-tithed.

16. Julie Bort, "Bill Gates Talks About the Heartbreaking Moment that Turned Him to Philanthropy," *Business Insider*, January 21, 2015, http://www.businessinsider.com/why-bill-gates-became-a-philanthropist-2015-1.

17. C. S. Lewis, *Mere Christianity* (New York: HarperCollins, 1980), 144–45.

18. Dan Olson, "The Time Is Ripe for Radical Generosity," *The Gospel Coalition* (blog), December 26, 2014, https://www.thegospelcoalition.org/article/the-time-is-ripe-for-radical-generosity.

19. Brian Solomon, "Meet David Green: Hobby Lobby's Biblical Billionaire," *Forbes*, September 18, 2012, https://www.forbes.com/sites/briansolomon/2012/09/18/david-green-the-biblical-billionaire-backing-the-evangelical-movement/#7937627b5807.

20. Jim Dwyer, "'James Bond of Philanthropy' Gives Away the Last of His

Fortune," *New York Times*, January 5, 2017, https://www.nytimes.com /2017/01/05/nyregion/james-bond-of-philanthropy-gives-away-the -last-of-his-fortune.html.

21. Tim Worstall, "Astonishing Numbers: America's Poor Still Live Better than Most of the Rest of Humanity," *Forbes*, June 1, 2013, https://www .forbes.com/sites/timworstall/2013/06/01/astonishing-numbers-americas -poor-still-live-better-than-most-of-the-rest-of-humanity/#53f24e2054ef.

22. Quoted in Randy Alcorn, *Money, Possessions, and Eternity* (Carol Stream, IL: Tyndale, 2003), Kindle locations 8750–70.

23. Samantha Grossman, "Allow This Man to Remind You that People Can Be Surprisingly Generous," *Time*, April 21, 2015, http://time.com /3830073/new-york-city-subway-roses/.

Chapter 7: A Life of Integrity

1. See "Joey Prusak," CBS Minnesota, http://minnesota.cbslocal.com/tag /joey-prusak/.

2. Amy Rees Anderson, "Success Will Come and Go, but Integrity Is Forever," *Forbes*, November 28, 2012, https://www.forbes.com/sites /amyanderson/2012/11/28/success-will-come-and-go-but-integrity-is -forever/#626ab564470f.

3. *Oxford Dictionary*, s.v. "integrity," accessed June 26, 2017, https://en .oxforddictionaries.com/definition/integrity.

4. Stephen Covey, *The Seven Habits of Highly Effective People* (New York: Simon & Schuster, 2004), 157.

5. Rick Ezell, "Are You a Person of Integrity?" *Parenting Teens*, accessed June 22, 2017, http://www.lifeway.com/Article/Parenting-Teens-Are -You-a-Person-of-Integrity.

6. "Quotes by Will Rogers," Will Rogers Today, accessed July 14, 2017, http://www.willrogerstoday.com/will_rogers_quotes/quotes.cfm?qID=2.

7. John, "Warren Buffett Looks for These 3 Traits in People When He Hires Them," *Business Insider*, January 4, 2017, http://markets .businessinsider.com/news/stocks/what-warren-buffett-looks-for-in -candidates-2017-1-1001644066.

8. Quoted in Jerry White, *Honesty, Morality, and Conscience* (Colorado Springs: NavPress, 1996), 18–19.

9. Carey Nieuwhof, "5 Ways to Build Your Integrity," February 8, 2012, https://careynieuwhof.com/5-ways-to-build-your-integrity/.

10. Ezell, "Are You a Person of Integrity?"

11. Dorothy Twohig, "George Washington: The First Presidency," Washington Papers, accessed June 26, 2017, http://gwpapers.virginia.edu/history/articles/george-washington-the-first-presidency/.

12. Adapted from Richard C. Stazesky, "George Washington, Genius in Leadership," Washington Papers, accessed June 26, 2017, http://gwpapers.virginia.edu/history/articles/george-washington-genius-in-leadership/.

13. Robert Bolt, *A Man for All Seasons* (New York: Vintage Books, 1990), 140.

14. Pat Williams with Jim Denney, *Souls of Steel* (New York: FaithWords, 2008), 37–38.

15. Adapted from *Today in the Word*, March 1989, 40. First used in the sermon "The Fruit of the Spirit Is Faith," December 17, 1982, Shadow Mountain Community Church.

16. Anderson, "Success Will Come and Go, But Integrity Is Forever."

17. Rick Renner, *Sparkling Gems from the Greek*, vol. 2 (Tulsa: Institute Books, 2016), 80–81.

18. Os Guinness, *Impossible People* (Downers Grove, IL: InterVarsity, 2016), Kindle locations 257–65.

19. Adapted from her biography on the Helen Keller Foundation website, accessed June 26, 2017, http://helenkellerfoundation.org.

20. Williams, *Souls of Steel*, 38.

21. Bill Hybels, "But I'm an Exception!" *CT Pastors*, Spring 1988, accessed June 26, 2017, http://www.christianitytoday.com/pastors/1988/spring/8812037.html.

22. Adapted from a story by Brennan Manning, in William J. Bausch, *A World of Stories for Preachers and Teachers* (Mystic, CT: Twenty-Third Publications, 2004), 282.

Chapter 8: A Life of Humility

1. John Dickson, *Humilitas* (Grand Rapids: Zondervan, 2011), 26–27.

2. Pat Williams, *Humility* (Uhrichsville, OH: Shiloh Run, 2016), 37.

3. Reuters, "'I Am the Greatest:' Muhammad Ali in His Own Words," *Newsweek*, June 4, 2016, http://www.newsweek.com/i-am-greatest-muhammad-ali-own-words-466432.

4. Duane Elmer, *Cross-Cultural Servanthood* (Downers Grove, IL: InterVarsity, 2006), Kindle locations 167–79.

5. The ideas in this section originated in Jim McGuiggan, *The God of the Towel* (West Monroe, LA: Howard, 1997), 7.

6. Max Anders, *Holman New Testament Commentary: Galatians, Ephesians, Philippians, & Colossians* (Nashville: Broadman & Holman, 1999), Kindle locations 4475–79.

7. John Ortberg, *Life-Changing Love* (Grand Rapids: Zondervan, 1998), 141–42.

8. Peggy Noonan, *When Character Was King* (New York: Penguin, 2001), 187.

9. William Barclay, *The Gospel of Mark* (Louisville: Westminster John Knox, 2004), 224.

10. Mark Batterson, *Chase the Lion* (Colorado Springs: Multnomah, 2016), 67.

11. Williams, *Humility*, 93.

12. Ibid., 13.

13. John Stott, *Romans* (Downers Grove, IL: InterVarsity, 1994), 330.

14. Tim Chester, "The First Time I Met John Stott," *Tim Chester* (blog), July 28, 2011, https://timchester.wordpress.com/?s=stott&submit=Search.

15. Mitch Albom, "George W. Bush Gives Lesson in Laughing at Ourselves," *Detroit Free Press*, March 4, 2017, http://www.freep.com/story/sports/columnists/mitch-albom/2017/03/04/george-bush-lesson/98710424/.

Chapter 9: A Life of Self-Discipline

1. Steven Lawson, "Self-Discipline," *Tabletalk*, August 1, 2013, http://www.ligonier.org/learn/articles/self-discipline/.

2. William Backus, *Finding the Freedom of Self-Control* (Bloomington, MN: Bethany House, 1987), 36.

3. Adapted from Rick Warren, "Developing Biblical Self-Control," Pastor Rick's Daily Hope, May 21, 2014, http://pastorrick.com/devotional/english/developing-biblical-self-control.

4. David Mathis, "Self-Control and the Power of Christ," *Desiring God*, October 8, 2014, http://www.desiringgod.org/articles/self-control-and-the-power-of-christ.

5. Maria Szalavitz as quoted in Tara Schiller, "15 Things Only Self-Disciplined People Would Understand," *Lifehack*, accessed June 19, 2017, http://www.lifehack.org/articles/communication/15-things-only-self-disciplined-people-would-understand.html.

6. Taken from Schiller, "15 Things Only Self-Disciplined People Would Understand."

7. Fritz Ridenour, *How to Be a Christian Without Being Religious* (Minneapolis: Billy Graham Association, 1967), 55.

8. Daniel Akst, "Who's in Charge Here?" Wilson Quarterly, Summer 2006, http://archive.wilsonquarterly.com/essays/whos-in-charge-here.

9. Harry S. Truman, "Note of Judge Harry S. Truman, May 14, 1934," Harry S. Truman Library and Museum, https://www.trumanlibrary.org /whistlestop/study_collections/trumanpapers/psf/longhand/index.php ?documentVersion=both&documentid=hst-psf_naid735210-01.

10. Maxie Dunnam, *The Communicator's Commentary*, vol. 8 (Dallas: Word, 1982), 120.

11. Bradley Wright with David Carreon, "The Science of Sinning Less," *Christianity Today*, April 21, 2017, http://www.christianitytoday.com /ct/2017/may/science-of-sinning-less.html.

12. David Jeremiah, *Turning Toward Joy* (Colorado Springs: Cook, 2006), 133.

13. Mark Batterson, *Chase the Lion* (Colorado Springs: Multnomah, 2016), 114.

14. William Barclay, *The Gospel of Matthew*, vol. 1 (Philadelphia: Westminster, 1958), 323.

15. Donald S. Whitney, *Spiritual Disciplines for the Christian Life* (Colorado Springs: NavPress, 1991), 20.

16. Wright, "The Science of Sinning Less."

17. Brian Feldman, "Matthew McConaughey Gave Exactly the Speech You'd Expect from Him," *Atlantic*, March 3, 2014, https://www .theatlantic.com/entertainment/archive/2014/03/matthew -mcconaughey-gave-exactly-speech-youd-expect-him/358728/.

18. H. A. Dorfman quoted in Schiller, "15 Things Only Self-Disciplined People Would Understand."

19. William H. McRaven, *Make Your Bed* (New York: Hachette, 2017), 97–99.

Conclusion

1. Adapted from "Power Outage Creates 'Cruise Ship from Hell,'" *Preaching Today*, accessed June 17, 2017, http://www.preachingtoday .com/illustrations/2013/september/7090913.html.

2. R. A. Torrey, *What the Bible Teaches* (Old Tappan, NJ: Fleming Revell, 1898), 289.

3. Quoted in Christopher J. Wright, *Cultivating the Fruit of the Spirit* (Downers Grove, IL: InterVarsity, 2017), Kindle location 64.
4. Charles Caldwell Ryrie, *The Holy Spirit* (Chicago: Moody, 1965), 99.
5. Adapted from George MacDonald as told in C. S. Lewis, *Mere Christianity* (New York: Macmillan, 1952), 160.

ABOUT THE AUTHOR

David Jeremiah is the founder of Turning Point, an international ministry committed to providing Christians with sound Bible teaching through radio and television, the Internet, live events, and resource materials and books. He is the author of more than fifty books, including *Is This the End?*, *The Spiritual Warfare Answer Book*, *David Jeremiah Morning and Evening Devotions*, *Airship Genesis Kids Study Bible*, and *The Jeremiah Study Bible*.

Dr. Jeremiah serves as the senior pastor of Shadow Mountain Community Church in San Diego, California, where he resides with his wife, Donna. They have four grown children and twelve grandchildren.

stay connected to the teaching series of

DR. DAVID JEREMIAH

• • • • • • • •

Publishing | Radio | Television | Online

FURTHER YOUR STUDY OF THIS BOOK

· · · · · · · ·

A Life Beyond Amazing Resource Materials

To enhance your study on this important topic, we recommend the correlating audio message album, study guide, and DVD messages from the *A Life Beyond Amazing* series.

Audio Message Album

The material found in this book originated from messages presented by Dr. David Jeremiah at Shadow Mountain Community Church, where he serves as senior pastor. These eleven messages are conveniently packaged in an accessible audio album.

Study Guide

This 144-page study guide correlates with the messages from the *A Life Beyond Amazing* series by Dr. Jeremiah. Each lesson provides an outline, an overview, and group and personal application questions for each topic.

DVD Message Presentations

Watch Dr. Jeremiah deliver the *A Life Beyond Amazing* original messages in this special DVD collection.

To order these products, call us at 1-800-947-1993
or visit us online at www.DavidJeremiah.org.

ALSO AVAILABLE FROM DAVID JEREMIAH

· · · · · · · ·

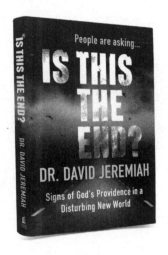

People Are Asking ... Is This the End?
by Dr. David Jeremiah

Never have the headlines been this jarring, the cultural changes this rapid, or the moral decay this pronounced. What on earth is happening? After each new occurrence, the most oft-heard questions are, "Will the world ever be the same again?" and "Where is God in all of this?"

Over the last few decades, Dr. David Jeremiah has become one of the world's most sought-after Christian leaders on topics that deal with biblical application and modern culture. And few would dispute that the pace at which things are currently changing is unprecedented. "The time has come to accept this new normal," Jeremiah says, "and understand how God's hand is still at work on His eternal plan for mankind."

We can better understand the greater story and the role we each play in this changing world. From prophetic clues in Scripture to an understanding of the power of Christ in all believers, this book directs us on a clear path forward.

Revealing the Mysteries of Heaven
by Dr. David Jeremiah

- What happens when we die? Where do we go?

- Is there an afterlife?

- Does the Bible say anything specific about heaven?

- Are there really streets of gold there? Pearly gates?

- Has anyone been to heaven and returned with insider information?

We all have questions about heaven, and many of us assume that we can't know the answers. But nothing could be further from the truth. God's Word is full of detailed information about heaven, if we only know where to look.

Dr. David Jeremiah wants you to understand this pivotal piece of God's plan for your life. In this new book, he uncovers the answers to your pressing questions about heaven, showing you how what you believe about heaven today affects every part of your faith and Christian life.

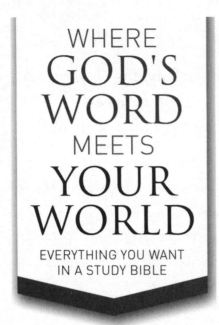

WHERE
GOD'S
WORD
MEETS
YOUR
WORLD

EVERYTHING YOU WANT
IN A STUDY BIBLE

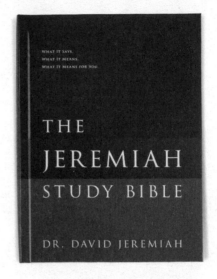

WHAT IT SAYS.
WHAT IT MEANS.
WHAT IT MEANS FOR YOU.

THE
JEREMIAH
STUDY BIBLE

DR. DAVID JEREMIAH

MORE THAN 100,000 PEOPLE
ARE USING *THE JEREMIAH STUDY BIBLE*

The Jeremiah Study Bible is comprehensive, yet easy to understand.
More than forty years in the making, it is deeply personal and designed
to transform your life. No matter your place or time in history, Scripture
always speaks to the important issues of life. Hear God speak to you
through studying His Word in *The Jeremiah Study Bible*.

NOW AVAILABLE IN:

- New King James Version
- Large Print NKJV
- New International Version

Request your Study Bible today:
www.DavidJeremiah.org/JSB

Stay Connected

· · · · · · · ·

Take advantage of two great ways to let
Dr. David Jeremiah give you spiritual direction every day!
Both are absolutely free!

① *Turning Points* Magazine and Devotional

Each magazine features:

- A monthly study focus
- 48 pages of life-changing reading
- Relevant articles
- Special features
- Devotional readings for
  each day of the month
- Bible study resource offers
- Live event schedule
- Radio & television information

② Your Daily Turning Point E-Devotional

Start your day off right!
Receive a daily e-devotional
from Dr. Jeremiah that will
strengthen your walk with God
and encourage you to live the
authentic Christian life.

Request your devotions today:

CALL: (800) 947-1993

CLICK: DavidJeremiah.org/Magazine

Books Written By David Jeremiah

• • • • • • • •

Escape the Coming Night

Count It All Joy

The Handwriting on the Wall

Invasion of Other Gods

Angels: Who They Are and How They Help . . . What the Bible Reveals

The Joy of Encouragement

Prayer: The Great Adventure

Overcoming Loneliness

God in You

Until Christ Returns

Stories of Hope

Slaying the Giants in Your Life

My Heart's Desire

Sanctuary

The Things That Matter

The Prayer Matrix

31 Days to Happiness: Searching for Heaven on Earth

When Your World Falls Apart

Turning Points

Discover Paradise

Captured by Grace

Grace Givers

Why the Nativity?

Signs of Life

Life-Changing Moments with God

Hopeful Parenting

1 Minute a Day: Instant Inspiration for the Busy Life Grand Parenting—
Faith that Survives Generations

In the Words of David Jeremiah

What in the World Is Going On?

The Sovereign and the Suffering

The 12 Ways of Christmas

What to Do When You Don't Know What to Do
Living with Confidence in a Chaotic World
The Prophecy Answer Book
The Coming Economic Armageddon
Pathways: Your Daily Walk with God
What the Bible Says About Love, Marriage, and Sex
I Never Thought I'd See the Day
Journey: Your Daily Adventure with God
The Unchanging Word of God
God Loves You: He Always Has—He Always Will
Discovery: Experiencing God's Word Day by Day
What Are You Afraid Of?
Destination: Your Journey with God
Answers to Questions About Heaven
Answers to Questions About Spiritual Warfare
Answers to Questions About Adversity
Quest: Seeking God Daily
The Upward Call
Ten Questions Christians Are Asking
Understanding the 66 Books of the Bible
A.D.: The Bible Continues: The Revolution That
Changed the World
Agents of the Apocalypse
Agents of Babylon
Reset: Ten Steps to Spiritual Renewal
People Are Asking ... Is This the End?
Hope for Today
Hope—An Anchor for Life
30 Days of Prayer
Revealing the Mysteries of Heaven

To order these books, call us at 1-800-947-1993 or
visit us online at www.DavidJeremiah.org.